T3-BED-379

*The Joy
Of Intimacy
With God*

Other books by J. Dwight Pentecost . . .

Designed To Be Like Him

A Faith That Endures (Hebrews)

The Joy of Intimacy With God (1 John)

The Joy of Living (Philippians)

The Parables of Jesus

Prophecy for Today

Things to Come

Thy Kingdom Come

Will Man Survive?

The Words and Works of Jesus Christ

A Harmony of the Words and Works of Jesus Christ

Your Adversary, the Devil

Discovery
House
PUBLISHERS

BOX 3566 · GRAND RAPIDS, MI 49501

*PUBLISHING BOOKS THAT FEED
THE SOUL WITH THE WORD OF GOD.*

A BIBLE STUDY GUIDE TO 1 JOHN

The Joy Of Intimacy With God

J. DWIGHT PENTECOST

with study questions by Jane Vogel

The Joy Of Intimacy With God
A Bible Study Guide to 1 John
Copyright © 1995 by J. Dwight Pentecost

Discovery House Publishers is affiliated with RBC Ministries, Grand Rapids, Michigan 49512.

Discovery House books are distributed to the trade by Thomas Nelson Publishers, Nashville, Tennessee 37214.

Unless otherwise indicated, all Scripture quotations are from The Holy Bible, New King James Version. Copyright © 1979, 1980, 1982 by Thomas Nelson, Inc. Used by permission.

Library of Congress Cataloging-in-Publication Data

Pentecost, J. Dwight.
    [Joy of fellowship]
    The joy of intimacy with God : a Bible study guide to 1 John / by J. Dwight Pentecost.
        p.   cm.
    Originally published: The joy of fellowship. Grand Rapids : Zondervan Pub. House, © 1977.

    ISBN 1-57293-006-3

    1. Bible. N.T. John, 1st—Criticism, interpretation, etc.
2. Bible. N.T. John, 1st—Study and teaching. I. Title.
BS2805.2.P462   1995
227'.94'007—dc20   95-32309
                                            CIP

All rights reserved

Printed in the United States of America

95 96 97 98 99 00 / CHG / 10 9 8 7 6 5 4 3 2 1

Contents

Outline of 1 John

Preface

We were created with a need for intimacy, and we are restless and insecure until this becomes our living experience. As believers, we delight to be in intimate relationship with fellow Christians. And we long to enter into an increasingly intimate relationship with the Father and the Savior.

John wrote his first epistle because he wanted his spiritual children to enter into that life of intimate fellowship with the Father and Son that he had seen Jesus experience with His Father and into which the apostle himself had entered. It is my desire to enable you to enjoy that same life of fellowship.

This book is intended for personal or group study. Questions at the end of each chapter are divided into three categories: "Starting Points" asks you to reflect on your personal situation and gives an opportunity for groups to share a little about themselves with one another; "Exploring the Text" focuses on the passage studied and its relationship to contemporary life; and "Where Do We Go From Here?" invites more specific personal and corporate application to daily living.

These studies have grown out of lectures given to the students at Dallas Theological Seminary and to the Grace Bible Church family in Dallas where I have served as pastor. They are put in this form to share the truths of 1 John with those who hunger both for a more intimate fellowship with the Father and the Son and for increasing fellowship with other believers. May the Lord use these studies to that end.

J. Dwight Pentecost

Lesson: 1

From the Beginning . . .

"Stand if you've ever locked your keys in your car," the speaker instructed.

Sheepishly, a handful of people in the audience stood, then took their seats again.

"Stand if you've ever eaten ice cream straight from the carton . . . forgotten your mother-in-law's birthday . . . driven the wrong way on a one-way street." At each statement, different members of the audience stood, then sat down again. The speaker gave one final instruction.

"Stand if you've ever felt alone in a crowd."

As one body, everyone in the audience rose.

Isolation is a scourge of modern society. Despite computer networking, global telecommunications, and the information superhighway, many people—all of us at one time or another—feel cut off from meaningful, intimate fellowship. Life may be busy, but too often it feels empty.

Jesus came that we might "have life, and have it to the full" (John 10:10, NIV). He came to share His life of oneness with the Father. As a branch is fruitful when it is connected to the vine, so our lives are fruitful when we are intimately connected to Jesus (John 15).

Meet John

John, the son of Zebedee, heard Jesus speak of abundant life. This young man was in partnership with his father and brother in a lucrative fishing business. Jesus appeared on the shores of Galilee and "saw two brothers, James the son of Zebedee, and John his brother, in a ship with Zebedee their father, mending their nets. He called them, and immediately they left the boat and their father, and followed Him" (Matt. 4:21–22). When John heard the Lord's summons he responded immediately and became a disciple, one of those who "believed in Him" (John 2:9–11). Shortly after this John attended a wedding feast where he saw Jesus transform water into wine (John 2:11).

When Jesus singled out twelve men from among the many disciples following Him, John was among them (Luke 6). Jesus called them apostles, or "sent ones." John, who had left his fishing business, was now sent out to reach men and to draw them to the Lord Jesus.

The Lord took John, together with Peter and James, "and went up on the mountain to pray. As he prayed, the appearance of His face was altered, and His robe became white and glistening" (Luke 9:28–29). John stood on the Mount of Transfiguration and saw the glory that belonged to the Lord Jesus from all eternity, a glory veiled by His flesh.

John sat at the Passover feast at which Jesus instituted the Lord's Supper. "Now there was leaning on Jesus' bosom one of His disciples, whom Jesus loved" (John 13:23).

At the Passover feast it was the custom of the Jews to recline on the left elbow on couches or pallets around a low table. So the one leaning on Jesus' bosom was at Jesus' right hand. The right hand was a place of honor. It was John who was appointed to a place of honor at the last Passover.

Jesus left the Upper Room and went to Gethsemane. There "He said to His disciples, 'Sit here while I pray.' And He took Peter, James, and John with Him" (Mark 14:32–33). John was in the shadows of the Garden when Jesus poured out His prayer to the Father, "If it is possible, let this cup pass from Me; nevertheless, not as I will, but as You will" (Matt. 26:39).

When Jesus went to Calvary, all the apostles abandoned Him, save one. From the cross Jesus saw His mother and the disciple He loved, and "He said to His mother, 'Woman, behold your son!' Then He said to the disciple, 'Behold your mother!' And from that hour that disciple took her to his own home" (John 19:26–27).

John was the first of the apostles to visit the empty tomb. Mary Magdalene went to anoint Jesus' body and saw the open grave.

> Then she ran and came to Simon Peter, and to the other disciple, whom Jesus loved, and said to them, "They have taken away the Lord out of the tomb, and we do not know where they have laid Him."
> Peter therefore went out, and the other disciple, and were going to the tomb. So they both ran together, and the other disciple outran Peter and came to the tomb first. (John 20:2–4)

John was intimately associated with the Lord Jesus Christ from the outset of His ministry until He rose from the dead. No other apostle shared so much of the heart of Jesus.

According to church tradition, John became shepherd of the flock in Ephesus. Now the aged apostle writes an epistle to his spiritual children to share what he has seen and heard of the abundant life.

John's Pastorate

The Ephesian church had a stormy history. The apostle Paul left a fruitful ministry in Greece to go to Ephesus, in the western portion of the Roman province of Asia, or Asia Minor (Acts 19). Ephesus was the social, economic, religious, cultural, and political center of that region.

Paul discovered some disciples of John the Baptist in Ephesus, people who believed John's promise that the Messiah was coming and were waiting for Him. No one had told them that the Messiah had already given His life as the Lamb of God, the sacrifice for the sins of the world. Paul singled out these disciples and opened up the Scriptures, explaining salvation through Christ, and with joy they embraced the Lord and entered into the body of Christ.

In the will and the wisdom of God, Paul settled in Ephesus for two years and carried on perhaps his most fruitful ministry there. We would conclude from his epistle to the Ephesians that Ephesus was the strongest church Paul established. But Paul knew from experience that, whenever he moved on to new people and new areas and left a church behind, the enemies of the cross of Christ would flood in and Satan would use false apostles to deceive these babes in Christ and divert them from the truth. So Paul warned the elders:

> Therefore take heed to yourselves and to all the flock, among which the Holy Spirit has made you overseers, to shepherd the church of God which He purchased with His own blood. For I know this, that after my departure savage wolves will come in among you, not sparing the flock. Also from among yourselves men will rise up, speaking perverse things, to draw away the disciples after themselves. (Acts 20:28–30)

Although the church had been forewarned, we learn from Paul's first letter to Timothy that false teachers did move in, perverting the thinking of the saints and dissuading the believers from following the true doctrine Paul had presented to them. These believers were brought under the crushing load of legalism and into bondage to the traditions of men. As a result they lost the liberty that belongs to the children of God. How Paul must have grieved!

When he wrote to the Philippians, Paul promised to visit them after his release from prison. Paul honored that commitment, but he wrote to Timothy, "Remain in Ephesus that you may charge some that they teach no other doctrine, nor give heed to fables and endless genealogies, which cause disputes rather than godly edification which is in faith" (1 Tim. 1:3–4). Paul charged Timothy to correct false teaching and expel the false teachers. He wrote two epistles to Timothy to encourage him in this work of bringing these believers back into the glorious liberty that belonged to the sons of God.

We learn how effective Timothy was from the book of Revelation. Writing to the seven churches, John records Christ's words to Ephesus: "I know your works, your labor, your patience, and that you cannot bear those who are evil. And you have tested those who say they are apostles and are not, and have found them liars; and you have persevered and have patience, and have labored for My name's sake and have not become weary" (Rev. 2:2–3). Christ can commend the Ephesian Christians because they have been brought back from the crippling legalism superimposed on them by false apostles.

A New Kind of Life
1 John 1:1–2

John's first epistle begins, "That which was from the beginning, which we have heard, which we have seen with our eyes, which we have looked upon, and our hands have handled, concerning the Word of life—" (v. 1). Many read this verse as though it says, "The One who was from the beginning. . . ." But this letter was not written to present the person of Christ; John had already done that in his gospel.

John's gospel begins, "In the beginning was the Word, and the Word was with God, and the Word was God. He was in the beginning with God" (John 1:1–2). John affirms Christ's deity, eternalness, and His distinctness as a Person in the Trinity. John introduces Christ as Creator and Revealer, for all things were made by Him and He is the Light of the world. Then, under the inspiration of the Holy Spirit, John presents a number of Christ's miracles to establish that He is the eternal Son of God. John presents the facts clearly and forcefully so that men may believe on Him.

Now, in his letter, John shares truths concerning abundant life in Christ. So verse 1 should be understood this way: "That unique kind of life which was from the beginning, which we have heard, which we have seen, which we have looked upon, and our hands have handled, we declare to you." A new kind of life available to believers!

Christ had taught and demonstrated the abundant life. So John shares what Christ shared with him while on earth.

First, he shares "that which we have heard." The Lord Jesus Christ revealed the Father with words He spoke to the disciples about the Father and about His relationship to the Father.

Second, Jesus translated words into deeds. So John saw the abundant life of God reproduced in Jesus Christ—"which we have seen with our eyes."

Third, John shares what "we have looked upon." "Looked upon" means "to give attention to," "to reflect on," so as to assimilate mentally. John had come to understand the meaning of the abundant life through his long and intimate association with Christ. John did not fully understand what Christ meant when He first spoke about sharing His life with believers, but as John lived with Christ and saw His relationship to the Father, the Spirit illuminated his mind so that he understood Christ's pronouncement, "I have come that they might have life, and that they might have it more abundantly" (John 10:10).

Finally, the apostle addresses what "our hands have handled." When he refers to the hands, he implies appropriating or making something one's own. What Christ taught and lived, John made his own, with the result that he possessed the abundant life.

John's writings emphasize several truths. First, Jesus claimed to be holy. He offered Himself as God come in the flesh. Surrounded by His enemies, Christ challenged them, "Which of you convicts Me of sin?" (John 8:46) If one of Jesus' enemies had been able to point to a single infraction of the Mosaic Law, they would have silenced Him forever, but Jesus was sinless and so His enemies stole away. In chapters one and two of his epistle, John writes about Christ's life. He reminds us that God is light—that is, absolute holiness—and he shows the demands that this holiness makes on one who would enter into that abundant life.

Second, Christ manifested love. He told His disciples how much He loved them and the world: "Greater love has no one than this, than to lay down one's life for his friends" (John 15:13). Jesus loved God the Father, He loved sinners, and He loved those who loved Him. In this epistle John reminds us that God is love and that we, too, have a responsibility to love. This is developed in chapters three and four.

Third, Jesus was obedient to the will of God. He testified, "I always do those things that please Him" (John 8:29). John was in the Garden when Jesus registered His complete obedience to the Father. Christ's obedience is reflected in the fifth chapter of John's epistle, where he shares the implications of Christ's obedience for the child of God who would enter into the fullness of life.

Fullness of Joy
1 John 1:3–4

A blind person has difficulty translating someone's description of an object into a mental picture. Humankind has difficulty understanding Jesus' description of His Father. The human mind is darkened to God's power and deity revealed in creation. If that darkness is to be dispelled, we must learn from the Lord Jesus Christ what the Father is like. The Son translated the life of the Father into a life lived before men so that they could come to know the Father.

John writes, "That which we have seen and heard we declare to you, that you also may have fellowship with us: and truly our fellowship is with the Father and with His Son Jesus Christ" (1 John 1:3). John is not writing to heal a breach when he says, "That you also may have fellowship with us." John refers to his readers over and over as his children; there was no estrangement between John and the Ephesians. He is writing so that they might enjoy the same fellowship with the Father and the Son that he and the other apostles enjoyed. To paraphrase verse 3: "That which we have seen and heard about this abundant life we declare to you that you also may enjoy the same fellowship in this life that we do."

We are sometimes envious of those twelve men our Lord chose to be with Him. We would love to have stood where John stood, to see the Lord Jesus touch a blind eye so that sight is restored, or touch a casket and see the dead rise. We are envious that they heard our Lord teach them about the Father and the abundant life He had come to share with them. We somehow feel that we would be far ahead spiritually if we had seen Christ with our own eyes. But, although the apostles saw Christ's deeds and heard His teachings, they did not understand them until after the Resurrection. We have the same capacity to enter into the abundant life available in Jesus Christ as any one of the disciples.

John explains this fellowship in the latter part of the third verse. "Our fellowship is with the Father and with His Son Jesus Christ." The word translated fellowship has in it the idea of having something in common. When two strangers are together in a situation where conversation seems necessary, they begin to probe to find some point of contact. "Where are you from?" "Where did you go to school?" "What is your hobby?" A barrier separates the two until they find some point of contact.

Before an individual can have fellowship with the Father and the Son, there must be some mutual point of contact. This is why God created people as He did.

Then God said, "Let Us make man in Our image, according to Our likeness; let them have dominion over the fish of the sea, over the birds of the air, and over the cattle, over all the earth and over every creeping thing that creeps on the earth." So God created man in his own image; in the image of God created He him. (Gen. 1:26–27)

Four times we read that God created humankind in His own image. Humanity was the capstone of all of God's creative work. Humankind reflects God's person.

God possesses the capacity of intellect to such an infinite degree that He knows all things. He possesses the capacity of emotion; so John could write, "God so loved the world that He gave His only begotten Son." God possesses a will with which He can choose and act—He is sovereign. God has no deficiencies in His personality, and He possesses all of these capacities to an infinite degree.

When God created Adam, He did not make an animal, He made a person. God gave Adam a mind to receive truth and to respond to that truth and know God. He gave Adam emotions so that he could receive the love of God and respond to God. He gave Adam a will so that when he received a revelation of the will of God he might respond and submit to the will of God. Adam had to a limited degree the same capacity that God possessed in infinite degree. Adam was in perfect fellowship with God.

But Adam disobeyed, and darkness settled on his mind so that he could not understand the truth of God; his emotions were degraded so that he could not love God; and his will was deadened so that he could not obey God. Adam lost all point of contact, so that fellowship between Adam and the Creator was impossible.

To make fellowship possible, the ___ came into this world to make huma___ creation. God imparts to the one wh___ as personal Savior a new mind so tha___ can understand and respond to the tr___ gives a new capacity of emotion so th___ can receive and respond to the love of God. He gives a new will so that the believer can receive a revelation of the will of God and obey the will of God. John is speaking of the response of the total person to the total person of the Father and the Son.

John shares again in verse 4 his reason for writing. "And these things we write to you that your joy may be full." John knows that the only true joy a child of God can experience is the joy that comes from being rightly related to the Father and the Son. This joy is exemplified by the Lord Jesus Christ.

Christ's joy did not come from this world's goods. He warned those who wanted to be His disciples: "Foxes have holes and birds of the air have nests, but the Son of man has nowhere to lay His head" (Matt. 8:20). Jesus lived on a subpoverty level. He slept in the homes of those who extended hospitality. When it came time to pay taxes, the Lord Jesus sent Peter to catch a fish and there find a coin to pay the taxes of two people. Yet Jesus knew infinite joy.

The world never heaped accolades on Jesus. His own people called Him a blasphemous traitor. He was not a business success. He was not a free man, for He was born among people enslaved to Rome. His joy resulted from being one with the Father and possessing the life of the Father.

As John's children look for spiritual satisfaction, they will not find it in what they accomplish or acquire. They will find joy in relationship with God, the source of abundant life.

ꜱTIONS FOR REFLECTION AND DISCUSSION

Starting Points

1. Imagine that a non-English-speaking person observed your church for a month. In what situations would he encounter the term *fellowship*? Based on his experiences, what definition of *fellowship* might he develop?

2. When have you experienced intimacy with God in a significant way? What did that experience mean to you?

Exploring the Text

3. If you were writing sales copy for the book of 1 John, what elements of John's life would you include in the section "about the author"? How did those experiences equip John to be used in the writing of this epistle?

4. What parallels do you see between the church at Ephesus and the Christian church today? Between the church at Ephesus and your own congregation?

5. How would you summarize the distinction between the purpose of John's gospel and John's first epistle?

6. What does John mean by *fellowship* in these verses?

7. In what misguided ways do people try to find joy? Make up some bumper-sticker slogans to reflect the things people pursue: "_____ can't buy you joy." What is true joy?

Where Do We Go From Here?
8. In what ways are you personally most likely to be sidetracked from finding true joy? (For example, finding satisfaction in your accomplishments? In your acquisitions?) What do you need to do to refocus?

9. Look over the "points of contact" described between the Creator and those created in His image. In which areas do you need a tune-up? How can you respond more fully to God with your mind, emotion, and will?

• •

Lesson: 2

Walking in the Light

If you have a small child in your house, you almost certainly also have at least one night-light—maybe several. A light in the bedroom keeps the monsters under the bed at bay. A light in the hallway shows the all-important path to the bathroom or, in the case of a thunderstorm, Mom and Dad's bedroom. A light in the bathroom makes that trip for a nocturnal drink of water easier and safer. Children are wise about light and darkness; they know that light is better.

Light has properties that help us understand God's holiness and His fellowship with humankind. First of all, light reveals. If something is lost, you use light to find it. When God's revelation to humankind was lost because of the blindness of the natural mind, Jesus Christ came as the Light, revealing the person of a holy God. John says, "No one has seen God at any time. The only begotten Son, who is in the bosom of the Father, He has declared Him" (John 1:18).

Light also purifies. I remember when our family doctor told us it was no longer necessary to keep my brother in isolation. I could move back into the room we shared. How I dreaded returning to a room once contaminated by scarlet fever! The doctor said we should take every item in the room out into the sunlight; so I helped my mother carry mattresses, carpets, drapes, and empty drawers down the stairs and outside where we spread them on the grass. After these items had been purified by the light of the sun, I was able to lie down and sleep in that room without fear of contamination.

It is also the peculiar property of light that it cannot be contaminated. There is no such thing as dirty light. Some of the sunlight may not be able to enter a room because the window is dirty, but the light that does pass through will not be affected by the dirt. John is using an apt image to convey a God of perfection who cannot be defiled. He reveals and purifies the uncleanness in us, but He is not contaminated.

Finally, light also comforts. What parent has not been awakened in the middle of the night by the fearful cry of a child? The parent slips in and dispels the fear by turning on a light. The light brings comfort and rest. We knows only fear of the Almighty when we are ignorant of God and anticipate God's judgment. Jesus is the God of all comfort. The Lord Jesus Christ came to let the light of the knowledge of God shine in our hearts.

Fellowship and Holiness
1 John 1:5–7a

The hosts in heaven worship God continuously because of the perfection of His person. Isaiah saw the seraphim surrounding the throne of God and heard them saying, "Holy, holy, holy, is the LORD of hosts" (6:3). God Himself finds great delight in His perfection. His character is holy. His thought is holy. His speech is holy. His acts are holy. While God is worthy to be revered for each of His attributes, heaven magnifies Him above all because of the perfection of His person.

• •

It is impossible for such a God to receive into His presence those who do not measure up to His character. But God makes believers acceptable to Himself through Jesus Christ. However, God cannot fellowship with one who is redeemed unless that person is walking in holiness.

John begins writing to his children in the faith by reminding them of the holiness of God. To fellowship with the Father they must know the basis of fellowship, as revealed by Christ: "This is the message which we have heard from Him and declare to you, that God is light and in Him is no darkness at all" (v. 5). Darkness and light are diametrically opposed. Where light shines, there is no darkness. Where darkness is, there is no light.

John is using an image employed throughout Scripture to depict the absolute holiness of God. After creation by the word of God, the earth was without form and void, empty and useless, and "darkness was on the face of the deep" (Gen. 1:2). God banished the darkness by bringing light. "God said, 'Let there be light'; and there was light" (Gen. 1:3) That light did not originate in a heavenly sun, it originated in a Person, the person of the Creator.

In obedience to the command of God, Moses raised up the tabernacle, preparing and placing the furniture in accordance with God's revealed instructions. And the Holy of Holies was wrapped in darkness because God had given no instructions for illuminating the recesses of the tabernacle. God brought the light of His presence to dispel the darkness. When all was in order, "the cloud covered the tabernacle of meeting, and the glory of the LORD filled the tabernacle" (Exod. 40:34).

In obedience to his father's instructions, Solomon built a magnificent temple of costly hewn stones and overlaid with gold and encrusted with silver; but there is no record of a window in that edifice. Once again the light of God's holiness dispelled the darkness "for the glory of the LORD filled the house of the LORD" (1 Kings 8:11). The priests carried no lamp, for they walked in the light of the holiness of God.

In the first chapter of John's gospel the world is again wrapped in darkness—spiritual darkness. God had revealed Himself to men, but they had rejected the light to walk in darkness. They had become blind because they did not know God.

> All things were made through Him, and without Him nothing was made that was made. In Him was life, and the life was the light of men. And the light shines in darkness, and the darkness did not comprehend it. (John 1:3–5)

Jesus came into the world to dispel the darkness in the minds and hearts of men. He was "the true Light which gives light to every man coming into the world" (John 1:9).

Salvation through Christ, the Light, does not make fellowship with God automatic. "If we say that we have fellowship with Him, and walk in darkness, we lie and do not practice the truth" (1 John 1:6).

If God were to fellowship with us while we are in sin, He would involve Himself in our sin. The one who sits behind the wheel of the getaway car is as much a bank robber as his partner inside the bank holding the gun. Adam sinned and ran to hide in the shadow of a bush. God came to fellowship with Adam, but He did not go down into the shadows. He stood in the light and said, "Adam, where are you?" Adam was not restored to fellowship until God had killed an animal and covered Adam's nakedness with the skin and Adam's sin with the blood.

John makes clear that the prerequisite to fellowship is to walk in the light. "If we walk in the light as He is in the light, we have fellowship with one another" (v. 7). John is not talking about the fellowship of two believers. He is referring to a believer in fellowship with the Father and the Son. The believer must be living in the light of the holiness of God, without any flaw in thought or word or deed, to fellowship with the Father and the Son. Our *salvation* does not depend on our godliness, but our *fellowship* with the Father does.

A holy God cannot tolerate sin. To know the blessing of fellowship with God and then step into darkness and walk alone is to rob yourself of joyful companionship with the Lord.

The Value of the Blood of Christ
1 John 1:7b–10

The heart of the believer confirms the testimony of Scripture—we were born in sin, we have practiced sin, and, even though we have been redeemed, we still have the capacity to sin. How can a holy God fellowship with a redeemed child who does sin? John comes face to face with this problem in his epistle.

Fellowship with God is possible because of the lasting worth of the blood of Jesus Christ. The blood of Jesus Christ keeps on cleansing us from all sin.

Throughout Scripture God reveals the redemptive value of blood. When the children of Israel were in bondage in Egypt, God fulfilled His promise and delivered them. God sentenced all of the firstborn in Egypt to death: "For I will pass through the land of

Egypt on that night, and will strike all the firstborn in the land of Egypt, both man and beast" (Exod. 12:12).

God also provided an escape from that universal death sentence: "Now the blood shall be a sign for you on the houses where you are, and when I see the blood, I will pass over you; and the plague shall not be on you to destroy you when I strike the land of Egypt" (Exod. 12:13). Those who believed God placed the blood of a lamb on their doorposts. The blood brought God's protection to that household. The word translated "pass over" here carries with it the idea "to hover over"; in other words, "When I see the blood, I will hover over you." God, the judge, now became the protector against the death angel. The death angel passed by because God was there to turn him aside. The blood brought a deliverer who charged Himself with the responsibility of protecting one who was under judgment.

The writer of Hebrews speaks of the value of blood: "According to the law almost all things are purified with blood, and without shedding of blood there is no remission" (Heb. 9:22). The writer recalls a ritual in the Day of Atonement.

On the Day of Atonement the high priest entered the Holy of Holies with the blood of an animal sacrifice and sprinkled the blood on the mercy seat. Above the mercy seat dwelt the Shechinah glory of God, the visible sign of God's presence among His people. Beneath the mercy seat in the Ark was the Law given to Moses. The Law had been broken, necessitating a blood sacrifice. So the blood on the mercy seat was between God and a broken law, literally covering sin.

God had designated appropriate sacrifices for the Israelite who had sinned in ignorance, but no prescribed sacrifice exonerated the Israelite guilty of premeditated sin. What a relief, then, that the child of God who had sinned willfully could remind God that the blood was on the mercy seat and then ask God's forgiveness.

David had sinned heinously, but he confessed his sin when he prayed:

> Have mercy upon me, O God, according to Your lovingkindness; according to the multitude of Your tender mercies, blot out my transgressions. Wash me thoroughly from my iniquity, and cleanse me from my sin. For I acknowledge my transgressions, and my sin is always before me." (Ps. 51:1–3)

Then he pleaded, "Purge me with hyssop, and I shall be clean; wash me, and I shall be whiter than snow" (Ps. 51:7). On the Day of Atonement the high priest used a hyssop branch to sprinkle the blood on the mercy seat. David pleaded that this blood cover his sin. Later he joyfully sang, "Blessed is he whose transgression is forgiven, whose sin is covered" (Ps. 32:1).

In obedience to the will of God, the sinless, eternal Son of God shed His blood to cover sin forever. A literal translation of 1 John 1:7 reads, "The blood of Jesus Christ, God's Son, keeps on cleansing us from all sin." Though it was shed nearly two thousand years ago, the blood of Christ has full power to cleanse. Fellowship with God is possible because of the lasting worth of the blood of Jesus Christ.

Some might say that fellowship with God is possible because man has lost his sin nature. A pastor told me of a man who said, "Pastor Mullen, I have not sinned in thirty years." The pastor gasped, "You haven't sinned in thirty years?" "No, I haven't."

Mullen replied, "Brother, keep it up for four more years and you'll have preeminence in heaven, because the Lord Jesus only lived thirty-three years without sinning."

John denies that we attain a state of perfection in this life. Paraphrasing verse 8, we read: "If we say that we no longer have a sin nature, we deceive ourselves, and the truth is not in us." Satan would like us to believe that we are beyond his power to tempt, and thus become easy prey when we let down our guard. The sin nature is ever with us. Fellowship with the Father is not the result of attaining a state of holiness in this life.

Paraphrasing verse 10 reveals a second misconception. "If we say that what we did was not really sin, we make God a liar, and His Word is not in us." Some people see sin only in heinous wrongdoing such as murder or adultery, rather than in the waywardness that plagues most of us day after day. But only God can define sin. Fellowship with the Father does not result from redefining sin and making God a liar by winking at anything unlike His absolute holiness.

The sinner is still a child of God, but sin has broken fellowship. My child may strain our relationship by disobeying, but he is still my child. Disobedience does not affect *position,* it affects fellowship. To be restored to fellowship with God, we must confess our sin: "If we confess our sins, He is faithful and just to forgive us our sins and to cleanse us from all unrighteousness" (1:9).

Confession is not generalizing before we drop off to sleep, "If I've done anything bad today, forgive me." The word *confess* means to say the same thing that God says about our sin. God points a finger at sin and says, "That was sin." When the Spirit of God illuminates our minds so that we judge our sin as God judges it, without making an excuse and without attempting to cover up, then we have made confession.

If believers confess their sin, God is faithful and just to forgive them. God is faithful to Himself and to His Word in that He places confessed sin under the blood of Christ. He is just in that He forgives His children's sins because of the everlasting value of the blood of Christ. God deals with sin on only one basis—the blood of Christ.

Our Advocate
1 John 2:1–2

The fact that Christ's blood restores us to fellowship doesn't make sin any less serious. So John writes, "My little children, these things write I to you, so that you may not sin" (2:1).

To protect us from underestimating the impact of our sin, John tells us what is involved when a believer sins. "If anyone sins, we have an Advocate with the Father, Jesus Christ the righteous. And He Himself is the propitiation for our sins, and not for ours only but also for the whole world" (2:1–2). John draws back the curtain of heaven to show what happens when a child of God sins.

"If anyone sins," might be translated, "While anyone is still in the act of sinning." The believer's sin causes activity in heaven that is beyond human comprehension. While anyone is in the act of sinning, he has an advocate with the Father, Jesus Christ the righteous. *Advocate* is the word still used in England meaning defense attorney. A defense attorney becomes necessary when someone has been charged with wrongdoing.

The sinning child of God has been accused. God the Father will not accuse the believer because the Father sees the believer not in his sin but in Jesus Christ.

> If God is for us, who can be against us? He who did not spare His own Son, but delivered Him up for us all, how shall He not with Him also freely give us all things? Who shall bring a charge against God's elect? It is God who justifies. (Rom. 8:31–33)

Jesus Christ is not the accuser, because "it is Christ who died, and furthermore is also risen, who is even at the right hand of God, who also makes intercession for us" (Rom. 8:34).

The accuser is identified in Revelation. In the great battle, "the great dragon was cast out, that serpent of old, called the Devil and Satan" (Rev. 12:9). A great voice announces, "The accuser of our brethren, who accused them before our God day and night, has been cast down" (Rev. 12:10). While Christ acts as our defense attorney, Satan stands before God as the constant accuser of the brethren.

Satan is engaged in a struggle for the soul. Every believer was born into Satan's kingdom and served him until God reached down in His infinite grace and delivered him from bondage to Satan and brought him into His family as His child. Satan resents that the believer has been wrested from his authority and control. Seeking to enslave the believer again, the devil uses God's words, "The soul who sins shall die" (Ezek. 18:4) and "The wages of sin is death" (Rom. 6:23). He has the effrontery to say, "Look at what that believer is doing. I demand You return him to me."

Because of the plea of the defense attorney, God does not deliver us to Satan. This Advocate does not enter a plea of innocence, nor does He plead for mercy. He pleads on the basis of His own blood.

John states that this Advocate is "the propitiation for our sins." The word *propitiation* means to cover over, to put under blood, just as the high priest did on the Day of Atonement when he sprinkled the blood of an animal sacrifice on the mercy seat. Jesus Christ has offered His own blood as a sacrifice to God. His blood is a cover, providing safety and refuge for those under His blood.

Now God is propitious, dealing with believers on the basis of that blood. As the defense attorney, Christ can plead His righteousness, for He became sin for us that we might be made the righteousness of God (2 Cor. 5:21). The perfection of His person is transferred to our account.

The blood of Christ is sufficient for all sins, for John adds, "He is the propitiation for our sins, and not for ours only but also for the whole world" (2:2). In the sight of God the blood of Christ is of such limitless value that it cannot be depleted. It is sufficient to cover every sin of every person who has lived or will live. We cannot exhaust the value of the blood of Christ by putting ourselves under its protecting covering again and again.

Obedience and Fellowship
1 John 2:3–6

The first epistle of John provides a test of our fellowship with God: "Now by this we know that we know Him, if we keep His commandments" (2:3). Obedience, then, determines whether we are in intimate fellowship with God the Father, God the Son, and God the Holy Spirit. Obedience is the basis of and the prerequisite to the believer's joy.

There can be no happiness or contentment in the home until children are in this right relationship to their parents. There can be no right relationship in the classroom until the pupils are in this relationship to the teacher. There can be no contentment in society until citizens are in this relationship to those who have been put in authority over them. There can be no peace and contentment in the business world until employees are in this relationship to their employer. And in the things of God, there can be no peace or contentment until those who are God's own are in subjection to His authority. God has ordained authorities, and authority requires submission, and submission involves obedience.

Since we are by nature rebels, a problem arises. It is that problem of inherent disobedience that John treats in this passage.

John first states this proposition negatively: "He who says, 'I know Him,' and does not keep His commandments, is a liar, and the truth is not in him" (2:4). If the believer claims that he is abiding in Christ but is disobedient to Christ's commandments, he is a liar. If a man says, "Lord Jesus, I love You for dying on the cross for me" but then disobeys Christ's teachings in Scripture, his actions prove him to be a liar. Disobedience always disrupts and destroys.

John then states the same proposition positively: "But whoever keeps His word, truly the love of God is perfected in him. By this we know that we are in Him" (2:5). If I am obeying the Word of God, then I am abiding with Christ.

The Lord Himself proclaimed this truth. "If anyone loves Me, he will keep My word; and My Father will love him and We will come to him and make Our home with him. He who does not love Me does not keep my words." (John 14:23–24). The test of fellowship with God, then, is what we do in obedience to His instructions in His Word. The believer who loves God wants to please Him.

Christ also reinforced this truth in somewhat different terms. "If you keep My commandments, you will abide in my love" (John 15:10). John has given us an example of what it is to live a life of obedience so that God can flood the life with joy. "He who says he abides in Him ought himself also to walk just as He walked" (1 John 2:6). If you want an example of a life of joy that is a result of complete obedience, there is only one place you can look, and that is to the Lord Jesus. The person who says he is abiding in Christ must be walking in complete obedience, as Jesus Christ walked.

How did Jesus walk? The Lord Jesus made a great affirmation when He said, "I am the light of the world. He who follows Me shall not walk in darkness, but have the light of life" (John 8:12). To follow Jesus is to walk in the light. A good illustration of this is found in John's gospel. Jesus stated, "I do always those things that please Him [the Father]" (John 8:29). Never in thought, or word, or deed had Jesus displeased the Father.

The world has its standards of conduct. People in high places believe they can live on a plane of morality radically different from the standard for which the rest of us hold ourselves responsible. When we adopt the standards of the world, we will never conform to God's holy demands. In the midst of the world's flexible standard is *the* inflexible standard of the Word of God, revealing the demands of God's absolute holiness. God fellowships with His children on the basis of His unalterable, holy character. "Thus says the Lord" is the basis of fellowship and the ground for the believer's joy.

QUESTIONS FOR REFLECTION AND DISCUSSION

Starting Points

1. Read again the properties of light described at the beginning of this chapter. As God's little child, when has God shone His light in your life in one of these ways? Why was it meaningful to you?

- ❏ Flashlight—revealing what is lost
- ❏ Sunlight—purifying what is contaminated
- ❏ Light through a dirty window—remaining uncontaminated
- ❏ Night-light—bringing comfort in the darkness

2. What is your initial reaction to this statement: "God cannot fellowship with one who is redeemed unless that person is walking in holiness" (p. 29)?

Exploring the Text

3. How does the Scripture background in this chapter add to your understanding of John's use of the imagery of *light?*

4. What is the relationship between holiness and fellowship with God? Between obedience and fellowship?

5. Summarize the significance of blood in Scripture. What role does blood play in bringing us into fellowship with God?

6. Two misconceptions about sin are mentioned on pages 33–34. What examples have you seen of these misconceptions in contemporary culture?

7. What is the relationship of confession to fellowship?

8. What is the practical value of Christ's work as Advocate for the believer? How is this a motivation not to sin?

Where Do We Go From Here?
9. "Obedience, then, determines whether we are in intimate fellowship with God" (1 John 2:3). According to this criterion, how intimate is your fellowship with God?

● ●

10. What role does confession play in your life? Where on the following scale do you usually find yourself?

Murmuring a general request for forgiveness before dropping to sleep.   ....   Judging my sin as God judges it without excuses.

11. (For personal reflection only.) What do you need to confess to God right now?

Lesson: 3

Love in All the Right and Wrong Places

"What the world needs now is love, sweet love." Or so the song goes. John would agree on the necessity of love, but that is where any similarity to a romantic crooner ends. The love he writes about is more sturdy than sweet, and as for lavishing it on "the world," well, depending on how you define your terms, that might very well be a case of misplaced affection.

Love and Fellowship
1 John 2:7–11

God reveals Himself in His Word as a God of love. To fellowship with a God of love, one must walk in love. In 1 John 2:3–6 the apostle writes that the intimate fellowship that will bring the believer into the fullness of joy depends first of all on obedience. Verses 7–11 relate that this intimate fellowship with the Father and the Son also depends on loving our brothers and sisters in Christ.

One of the fundamental postulates of the Mosaic Law was that the Israelites were to love one another. The Pharisees, a sect claiming to interpret the law of Moses, sent a hostile representative to test Jesus. The Pharisees had codified the Old Testament law into 365 prohibitions and 250 commandments, and a man supposedly discharged his responsibility to God by observing all of these.

One Pharisee challenged Christ: "If you are what you claim to be, sent from God, tell us what the greatest commandment in the law is." This was tantamount to asking Christ what the purpose of the law was, and how one fulfilled the demands of righteousness in the law. The Lord replied: " 'You shall love the LORD your God with all your heart, with all your soul, and with all your mind.' This is the first and great commandment. And the second is like it: 'You shall love your neighbor as yourself' " (Matt. 22:37–39).

When Jesus gathered His disciples around Him in the Upper Room, He said to them: "By this all will know that you are My disciples, if you have love for one another" (John 13:35). The people of Israel had many marks of identification. Circumcision indicated belief in God's covenant with Abraham. The disciples of the Pharisees were easily recognized because they placed portions of Scripture in little boxes tied to their foreheads or forearms. Those who identified themselves with John the Baptist received his baptism. Every one of these marks was external.

In the Upper Room the Lord told His disciples that He would give them an internal mark of identification. The mark would be their love for one another.

After saying that he was not writing a new commandment but an old commandment, John then speaks of "a new commandment" (1 John 2:8). This new commandment is the Old Testament instruction that the Lord Jesus Christ emphasized in the Upper Room when He said to His disciples, "This is my commandment, that you love one another" (John 15:12).

Building on the concept of loving one another, the apostle Paul speaks of love fulfilling the law (Rom. 13:8). Paul explains that those seeking the highest good of their brother will never transgress the law, for breaking of the law is never love. "Love does no harm to a neighbor; therefore love is the fulfillment of the law" (Rom. 13:10).

John makes it clear that fellowship with God depends on love for one another. Without love for one another there can be no love for God. And where there is no love for God there is no fellowship with the Father and the Son. The one who claims to be in the light but is hating his brother is actually in darkness. Such a person cannot under any circumstance be enjoying fellowship with God. Where there is hate, there is no fellowship. Where there is hate, there is no joy.

The love of which John speaks is not so much a manifestation of the emotions as it is a manifestation of the will. It is not first of all an emotional response to another person. It is an interest in, care for, and concern about another person. A key word in this matter is the word *commitment.* Loving the brother demands the commitment of a person to a person. When one believer shows care and concern about the total needs of a brother or sister in Christ as a person, he is fulfilling the obligation of Scripture to love.

Too often we conclude that if we write out a check to cover a brother's material needs we have discharged our obligation to him. That is but an insignificant part. A person can attend a church and can send his check to meet the bills and pay the salaries and maintain the properties and feel he has discharged his commitment to the church. All he has done is take care of housekeeping details. A church is not a group of people committed to a building or to an organization. When people become members of a church they are making a commitment to each other. And not until we exercise the responsibilities of that personal commitment one to the other are we functioning as a church. We must minister one to the other, bear one another's burdens, share one another's griefs, support one another in need, minister one to the other in love.

If I hurt and have deep needs, but out of pride I refuse to share those needs with you, what I am saying to you is, "I don't love you." And when we are acquainted with needs and refuse to respond, we are saying, "I don't love you." We cannot then enjoy fullness of fellowship with the Father and with the Son.

We like to withdraw into our own little circle and build a wall around ourselves. We can do that, but then we will not know the fullness of joy that comes from loving our brothers and sisters in Christ. "By this all will know that you are My disciples, if you have love for one another." If you would know the fullness of joy, love one another, and so fulfill the law of Christ.

To Young and Old
1 John 2:12–14

That the perfect God desires fellowship with His imperfect creatures is utterly astounding. This fellowship with the Father is not limited to one age group nor to one group who have reached a certain spiritual standing. John addresses these words to fathers, young men, and little children. Fellowship is possible from the youngest to the oldest.

John is also emphasizing that fellowship is not reserved for those who have come to spiritual maturity. It is not only for those who are fathers in the faith but also for those who are young in the faith and those who are newborn babes in Christ. This privilege of intimate fellowship with the Father is possible to any child of God.

First of all, John says, "I write to you, little children, because your sins are forgiven you for His name's sake" (v. 12). The word *forgive* means to remove, to erase, to put away. It has in it the idea of the separation of the sinner and his sin so that one is no longer identified with the other.

To one familiar with the Old Testament, this brings to mind the ritual of the Day of Atonement. On that annual feast day, observed by Israel according to the law, on behalf of the nation the high priest sacrificed two goats. When the first was slain, the high priest took the basin filled with blood into the Holy of Holies and sprinkled it on the mercy seat. The high priest then left the Holy of Holies and placed his hands on the head of the second goat, confessing the sins of the nation. Then he entrusted the animal to a man responsible to lead it into the wilderness.

As a member of the congregation saw the priest placing his hands on the head of the goat, he could think: "My sins are being transferred to a substitute. That goat is my sin-bearer." Then he would watch the animal being led out of the camp, and he could say, "The sins that I bore, that animal now bears, and he is bearing them away from me so that I no longer bear them." As he watched the man disappear over the horizon, he could say, "My sins have been removed; my sins are gone."

That separation of the sin from the sinner is the fundamental concept in the mind of the apostle when he says, "Your sins are forgiven you for His name's sake." John emphasizes that Jesus Christ came into this world specifically to make it possible for God to remove sin from the sinner. There is no happier message in the Word of God than this good news that our sins have been erased, not only from the *record* of God, but from the very *memory* of God. And because my sins have been forgiven, I can enjoy fellowship with God.

Second, in verse 13 and again in verse 14 John states, "I write to you, fathers, because you have known Him who is from the beginning." There is a vast difference between knowing *about* a person and knowing him personally. Jesus Christ came into this world to introduce the Father to us and introduce us to the Father, so that knowing the Father, we might enjoy fellowship with Him. Jesus emphasized the necessity of this introduction of the Father to us and us to the Father: "Nor does anyone know the Father except the Son, and the one to whom the Son wills to reveal Him" (Matt. 11:27). Were it not for the revelation that Jesus Christ has given to us, we might as well place over our church entrances the Greek superscription, "To the Unknown God."

Natural man does not come to know God by natural means. And natural man will never discover God and come to know Him so that he can enjoy Him. He may look at God's handiwork and be convinced that God exists and that He is a God of power who has arranged this universe, but he will never know Him personally. Jesus Christ came to make the unknown God known so we might enjoy fellowship with Him.

In his gospel John records Philip questioning Jesus:

> Philip said to Him, "Lord, show us the Father, and it is sufficient for us." Jesus said to him, "Have I been with you so long, and yet you have not known Me, Philip?

He who has seen Me has seen the Father; so how can you say, 'Show us the Father'? Do you not believe that I am in the Father, and the Father in Me? (John 14:8–10)

What John had learned about the Father from Jesus brought him into intimate fellowship with the Father. John had taught his spiritual children and they had come to know the Father. Fellowship is possible not only because sins are forgiven, but also because believers come to know God as their Father.

Third, John says, "You have overcome the wicked one" (vv. 13–14). The believer has come through the territory over which Satan reigns.

I once looked out my study window and saw our dachshund under the pecan tree in our side yard, leaping as high as her little three-inch legs would allow. She was barking and growling at a squirrel calmly eating nuts on one of the limbs, oblivious to any noise or danger. The squirrel was secure up there where no dachshund could ever go, but to get there it had to run across the lawn and climb to safety. Until up in the tree, it was in jeopardy. The believer finds safety and security where God has placed him.

Paul refers to this when he says God has "delivered us from the power of darkness and conveyed us into the kingdom of the Son of His love, in whom we have redemption through His blood, the forgiveness of sins" (Col. 1:13–14). When we enter into the blessings of sins forgiven, we are translated out of the kingdom of this world, the kingdom of Satan into which we had been born, and are lifted up into the kingdom of "His dear Son." All the ravages of Satan cannot dislodge us nor unsettle us.

Paul states in 2 Corinthians 2:14 that Christ always leads His own in His train of triumph. He is the Victor in a triumphal procession that will take

Him into glory, and He sweeps along in His train the multitudes who have received Him as Savior and have experienced the forgiveness of sin.

And we walk in His triumph. Because we are victors, we can enjoy fellowship with the Father. This intimate experience of enjoying the Father's presence is possible for us because our sins have been forgiven, because we have come to know the Father intimately through Jesus Christ, and because we have been lifted out of that sphere where no fellowship is possible and brought into the family of God.

Love for the World
1 John 2:15–17

We are to love God. We are to love one another. But John commands his spiritual children, "Do not love the world" (2:15).

The term *world* has three meanings in Scripture. At times it refers to the earth. God created the earth to reveal to humanity that He is God and the powerful Creator. The beauties of nature were designed to move our hearts toward God and remind us of a Maker who wants His creatures to enjoy His rich creation. First John 2:15 does not employ this meaning of *world*.

World frequently refers to the mass of humankind. But John is not forbidding love for the human race. Such a commandment would be contrary to God's character, for John 3:16 tells of a God who loves the world, the world of lost humanity, and who reached out in His love to provide a Savior. God would be countermanding His nature if believers were commanded not to love the mass of humankind whom He loves.

The most common use of the word *world* in Scripture is to refer to the kingdom of Satan, an organized system under satanic control. Paul states that Satan is the god of this kingdom (2 Cor. 4:3–4). The world under Satan submits to Satan's authority. First John 5:19 states, "We know that we [believers] are of God, and the whole world lies under the sway of the wicked one."

This world is characterized by darkness. Darkness in Scripture is the absence of light and light is the knowledge of God. Satan's kingdom must walk in darkness because the god whom they recognize has eclipsed all knowledge of God.

Satan, the god of this world of darkness, is working out his purposes through his subjects, and this always produces disobedience because Satan is a rebel who is opposed to God. As a result, his subjects are opponents of God who walk in disobedience (Eph. 2:1–2).

Christ characterized the world by its hatred of God:

> If the world hates you, you know that it hated Me before it hated you. If you were of the world, the world would love its own. Yet because you are not of the world, but I chose you out of the world, therefore the world hates you. (John 15:18–19)

Through the world system Satan executes his purpose. His goal is to dethrone God and enthrone himself as the god of this universe. He seeks to retain all who are presently in his kingdom and prevent them from entering the kingdom of God by a new birth. Satan attempts to reproduce himself in his children so that all the evil and the rebellion and the lawlessness that characterizes him is translated into action.

However, this world system is guilty before God; it has had judgment passed on it. In His holiness God has condemned the character and the conduct of the world. Paul writes, "Now we know that whatever the law says, it says to those who are under the law, that every mouth may be stopped, and all the world may become guilty before God" (Rom. 3:19). On the eve of His crucifixion Jesus looked at the cross and saw a divine judgment on a guilty world. "Now is the judgment of this world; now the ruler of this world will be cast out" (John 12:31). The judgment on this guilty world will be executed in God's own time.

John then gives three reasons why we are forbidden to love the world. First, "If anyone loves the world, the love of the Father is not in him" (1 John 2:15). A holy God cannot love sin, and if a child of God loves that which God hates, it is never God who is doing the loving through him and in him.

Next John focuses on the content of the world: "For all that is in the world—the lust of the flesh, the lust of the eyes, and the pride of life—is not of the Father but is of the world" (v. 16). "The lust of the flesh" is the evil inclination of human sinful nature. "The lust of the eyes" refers to Satan's tempting the natural man so that evil desire degenerates into lust or covetousness. "The pride of life" is the desire for prominence and adulation.

Satan used these three channels to assault Eve. First, the lust of the flesh: "The woman saw that the tree was good for food" (Gen. 3:6). Further, she saw "that it was pleasant to the eyes," a thing to be coveted. This is the lust of the eye. And it was "a tree desirable to make one wise," that is, the pride of life.

Satan also tempted Christ at the outset of His ministry through these three channels. He challenged Christ to make stones into bread—the satisfaction of the flesh. He showed Him the kingdoms of the world— the lust of the eye. He took Him to the pinnacle of the temple and challenged Him to demonstrate His faith—an appeal to the pride of life. Then Satan left Christ because there were no more channels through which to tempt Him.

John gives a third reason not to love the world: it is transitory. "The world is passing away, and the lust of it; but he who does the will of God abides forever" (v. 17). Satan's power is only for a time; God's power is for all time.

James uses very strong language to warn against befriending the world: "Adulterers and adulteresses! Do you not know that friendship with the world is enmity with God? Whoever therefore wants to be a friend of the world makes himself an enemy of God" (James 4:4). When we were first redeemed by the blood of Christ, we were brought into a love relationship with the Father and the Son. When one who has been knit to the heart of God loves what God hates, he is committing adultery against God.

QUESTIONS FOR REFLECTION AND DISCUSSION

Starting Points

1. Do you find it easier to offer demonstrations of Christian love or to receive them? Why are both important?

2. Think of—but don't name aloud!—someone you find difficult to love. What makes this person so unlovable to you?

Exploring the Text

3. How does viewing love as a manifestation of the will rather than a manifestation of the emotions color how you love your brothers and sisters in Christ?

4. Review the characteristics of brotherly love described on pages 45–46. What specific actions might demonstrate that kind of commitment and caring? What substitutes do people often mistakenly think fulfill their responsibilities to love others?

5. David echoed the imagery of the goat carrying his sin out of reach when he wrote, "As far as the east is from the west, so far has He removed our transgressions from us" (Ps. 103:12). What other contrasts can you think of that reflect that distance?

6. What things might a person know *about* God without really knowing God? What might be some warning signs that such a person doesn't yet know God? How did you get "introduced" to God?

7. What are some ways in which Satan tempts people today through the lusts of the flesh? The lusts of the eyes? The pride of life? What destructive results have you seen?

Where Do We Go From Here?

8. In what areas is Satan working to wean your love away from God and toward the world? Which of the three temptations listed in 1 John 2:16 do you encounter most? Can you find someone to encourage you and hold you accountable to resist those temptations?

9. In what concrete ways can you express love to a brother or sister in Christ this week?

Lesson: 4

Thinking Straight

My wife and I feel very close to a family in northern Wisconsin, even though we have seen them only once. We are drawn to them because their son married our daughter. Humankind, too, is drawn to God through a relationship to His Son. We know the Father because of what we know of the Son.

The apostle John emphasizes this great truth throughout the second chapter of his epistle—we have fellowship with the Father because of the Son. And the privilege of fellowshiping with the Father depends on what we think of His Son, Jesus Christ. That's why it's so important to get our thinking straight about who Jesus is—especially in a crooked world.

Antichrist and Crooked Thoughts
1 John 2:18–19

Because of the evil of the world, Satan's kingdom, John warns against the antichrist. The word *antichrist* can be understood in two ways. First, it can mean one who comes as a substitute for Christ. It refers to a person who will appear on the earth in the end time. This person will gain worldwide political and religious power that will constitute him as the world's ruler and god. This individual is described in Daniel 7, 8, 11; 2 Thessalonians 2; and Revelation 13, 17, where this person comes as a substitute for Christ. He is a false messiah whom the Lord will judge and destroy at His second advent to this earth.

John also uses the term *antichrist* in the sense of anyone who is opposed to Jesus Christ. John is anticipating the coming of the Antichrist, the lawless rebel who sets himself up as king and god, but he also tells that the antichrist philosophy is already operative in the world.

First, antichrist manifests itself in the religious realm. The Word of God clearly teaches that Jesus was born of a virgin in order to clothe His undiminished deity with complete humanity. These two were so inseparably united that the Lord Jesus Christ is God-man—God come in the flesh. All the teaching of the Word or God is based on this doctrine of the person of Jesus Christ.

The philosophy of Satan that permeates the religious world denies that Jesus Christ is the Son of God come in the flesh. John writes: "Who is a liar but he who denies that Jesus is the Christ?" (2:22) Later he says,

> By this you know the Spirit of God: Every spirit that confesses that Jesus Christ has come in the flesh is of God, and every spirit that does not confess that Jesus Christ has come in the flesh is not of God. And this is the spirit of the Antichrist, which you have heard was coming, and is now already in the world. (4:2–3)

Antichrist also operates in the political realm. Governments hinder the proclamation of the gospel, curb religious freedom, prevent public prayer, practice genocide, approve the murder of unborn children, legitimize promiscuity, and condone perverse practices.

The social realm is also affected by antichrist. Young people, for example, are growing up in what is commonly called the drug culture. The effect of drugs is to numb the work of the Holy Spirit in convicting people of sin and righteousness and judgment to come. A person either must face his sin and seek the righteousness of Christ so as to escape judgment or deaden the convicting voice of the Holy Spirit. Drugs are but one example of the elements in society that are in opposition to Jesus Christ.

Antichrist operates in the moral realm. The moralist says humankind is intrinsically good. All that is needed is to remove the restraints and make a man free and he will express his innate goodness. The moralist also claims there is no absolute standard of right and wrong. Experience determines what is right and wrong. Situational ethics says one can do anything the situation demands. Ignoring the standards of the holiness of God set down in the Word of God, people live like animals and call this acceptable conduct.

Antichrist has also pervaded the arts and manifests its opposition to Jesus Christ through music and art that is not designed to produce peace, harmony, and unity but rather lawlessness and rebellion.

Scripture speaks about our response to antichrist. The apostle Paul writes, "Come out from among them and be separate, says the Lord. Do not touch what is unclean, and I will receive you" (2 Cor. 6:17). Anything that manifests Satan's opposition to Christ is to be totally repudiated. It cannot be followed. We cannot conform to it and expect the blessing of God.

Those who are separate from the world must identify with Jesus Christ. Separation places one in a neutral zone. One who has separated himself from the antichrist system must identify with Jesus Christ if he is to be on the ground of God's blessing and victory. Separation *from* antichrist must be followed by separation *to* Jesus Christ.

We who are separated from antichrist and identified with Christ must walk in continuous dependence on the Word of God. We have an anointing from God in the person of the Holy Spirit, who interprets Scripture for us. The Holy Spirit of God also helps believers to interpret the world so that they understand how all areas of life are permeated by the spirit of antichrist.

Defense Against Deception
1 John 2:20–24a

When Satan assaults a person, he begins by attacking the mind. When he tempted Eve to disobey the command of God, he appealed to her mind: "Has God indeed said, 'You shall not eat of every tree of the garden'?" (Gen. 3:1).

First Line of Defense: Teaching of the Spirit
In 1 John 2:20–24 the apostle provides the defense against these attacks of Satan. The first defense is found in verse 20: "You have an anointing from the Holy One, and you know all things." Christ laid the foundation for this truth in His Upper Room discourse. On the eve of His crucifixion the Lord Jesus told His disciples of the new relationships they would enter with the Father and Son and the Spirit following His ascension. Three times that night the Lord spoke of the coming of the Holy Spirit.

First He promised that the Spirit would come. "I will pray the Father, and He will give you another Helper, that He may abide with you

forever—the Spirit of truth" (John 14:16–17). The
Lord Jesus had been their helper. But now He was
going away, and so the Lord promised that the
Father would send another Person like Himself to
be their helper.

In this discourse Jesus referred specifically to the
teaching ministry of the Holy Spirit. "But the
Helper, the Holy Spirit, whom the Father will send
in My name, He will teach you all things, and bring
to your remembrance all things that I said to you"
(John 14:26). While the Holy Spirit will help in
every need, the Lord focused on one of the
paramount needs of the children of God: the need
for a teacher who will help us understand Christ's
revelation of the Father and of Himself.

For more than three years the Lord had been
instructing His disciples, but they had not
understood much of His instruction. He had sowed
the seed, as it were, and the seed was lying dormant.
It did not come to fruit. But the Lord promised that
the Spirit would do two things. The Spirit would
cause the disciples to recall the very words that Jesus
had said, and then He would help them to
understand these words and enter into the truth.
Christ's teaching is living seed and that seed
maintains its life until the showers from heaven
bring it to fruit. None of the Lord's teaching was
wasted; He had been sowing.

In the same discourse the Lord spoke a third time
concerning the ministry of the Helper.

> When He, the Spirit of truth, has come, He will guide you
> into all truth; for He will not speak on His own authority,
> but whatever He hears He will speak; and He will tell you
> things to come. He will glorify Me, for He will take of
> what is Mine and declare it to you. (John 16:13–14)

The Spirit's primary ministry is to reveal the things of Christ so that believers might enter into intimate fellowship with Him.

After referring to the anointing of the Holy Spirit, John adds, "You know all things." John recognized that his spiritual children were once marked by a total inability to understand divine truth, but now they have a capacity to understand; they can respond in love to the truth that has been presented. When someone is born again, that person receives a new mind, the mind of Christ (1 Cor. 2:16). The Holy Spirit does not try to take the old darkened mind and let the light of the truth of God filter through. In regeneration the Holy Spirit gives us a new mind, a whole new capacity, that can understand and appropriate the truth of God.

John points out the antagonism between truth and error. These are mutually exclusive, and the Holy Spirit never moves in the realm of a lie. "I have not written to you because you do not know the truth, but because you know it, and that no lie is of the truth" (v. 21). John is remembering the words of Christ that Satan is a liar and the father of lies (John 8:44). Satan is a liar, not only because he tells lies, but because he deceives men concerning *the truth*. John presents Satan's lie: "Who is a liar but he who denies that Jesus is the Christ? He is antichrist who denies the Father and the Son. Whoever denies the Son does not have the Father either" (vv. 22–23).

The Spirit's principal work is to reveal the truth concerning the person of Jesus Christ. The test of any religious system is its response to the question, "Who is Jesus Christ?" The Word of God makes it unequivocally clear that Jesus Christ is the eternal Son of the eternal God, who came in the flesh to save sinners. Satan will never, under any circumstances, acknowledge that truth. Satan may concede that God by the spoken word created the universe and that the Bible is the Word of God, but Satan will never concede that Jesus Christ is the Son of God.

Every antichrist philosophy at work in the world today must deny that Christ is the Son of God. John says that antichrist, whether it manifests itself in the religious or the political or the moral or the social realm, will be evident through its denial of the person of Jesus Christ. The safeguard against this lie of Satan is the teaching ministry of the Holy Spirit.

Second Line of Defense: Roots in the Word
We have a second defense against the attacks of Satan, and this moves into the practical realm. John says, "Therefore let that abide in you which you heard from the beginning. If what you heard from the beginning abides in you, you also will abide in the Son and in the Father" (v. 24). The word *abide* means to get your roots down into something so that you are being nourished and sustained by that in which you are rooted. John is telling God's children that the truth revealed to them by the Holy Spirit will preserve them against the lies of Satan. Just as a plant puts roots down into the ground and is nourished by the soil, so the child of God puts roots down into the Word.

On the one hand we have the unceasing ministry of the Holy Spirit to teach us. On the other hand we have the ministry of Word to sustain us. The believer's relationship to the Word of God, as well as to the teaching ministry of the Spirit of God, determines to what degree he can stand against all of Satan's assaults on the mind.

The writer in Proverbs exhorts: "Keep your heart with all diligence, for out of it spring the issues of life" (Prov. 4:23). *Heart* used to refer to the seat of reason. Paul sounded the same note as the Old Testament writer: "For the weapons of our warfare are not carnal but mighty in God for . . . casting down arguments and every high thing that exalts itself against the knowledge of God, bringing every thought into captivity to the obedience of Christ" (2 Cor. 10:4–5). Paul recognizes that the believer is constantly being assaulted by antichrist. He must oppose and overthrow all these attacks on the mind by "bringing every thought into captivity to the obedience of Christ." The believer must hide the Word of God in his mind so that the teachings of Scripture are ever-present in his thinking.

What Do You Think of the Christ?
1 John 2:24b–29

During His earthly ministry Christ had sent the disciples throughout the land of Israel to proclaim His person and work. They announced that in fulfillment of prophecy God had sent His own Son as Savior and Lord. They returned to Christ to report on their ministry.

Christ did not ask how many meetings they had held. He did not want to know the attendance at the services. He asked about the response of the people. "Who do men say that I, the Son of man, am?" (Matt. 16:13).

Some of the disciples' listeners had said that Jesus was John the Baptist brought back to life. John had deeply impressed that generation, so it was high praise to be likened to John. Others thought that Elijah had returned to earth to minister again. Elijah had denounced sin in high places and called the people to repentance and warned them of the coming judgment. Some likened Jesus to Jeremiah, the prophet whose heart was broken as he saw the sin of his people inviting the judgment of God. Others could not identify Jesus but recognized that because He came with God's authority He must be one of the prophets. Christ's person and message were more than human phenomena. This was recognized across the land, but no one said that Jesus was the eternal Son of the eternal God become flesh.

Christ then asked, "Who do you say that I am?" Peter, as spokesman for all twelve, confessed the person and work of Christ when he cried out, "You are the Christ, the Son of the living God." The term *Christ* embraces the Old Testament prophecy that the Lamb of God would shed His blood to take away the sin of the world before He became the King who rules on earth. In calling Him Christ, Peter confessed his faith in Jesus' work. Peter also confessed his faith in Christ's person: "the Son of the living God."

If I think your child is a little monster and you are aware of my opinion, we will not get along together. My attitude toward your child affects your attitude toward me. John says that this is also true of God the Father. If the believer does not think well of the Son, the Father cannot receive him into the warmth of His fellowship, because God delights in His Son. He testified from heaven again and again, "This is My beloved Son, in whom I am well pleased."

The teaching ministry of the Spirit, which John again mentions in verse 27, interprets the things of Christ for the believer, making it possible for us to fellowship with the Son and through Him with the Father. It is impossible to fellowship with someone you don't know. Fellowship must be based on knowledge. And to make fellowship between the Father and the believer possible, God has sent the Holy Spirit to reveal the things of Christ.

John provides a test to determine what the believer thinks of the Son.

> And now, little children, abide in Him, that when He appears, we may have confidence and not be ashamed before Him at His coming. If you know that He is righteous, you know that everyone who practices righteousness is born of Him. (vv. 28–29)

We reveal our estimate of Jesus Christ by the degree to which we reproduce Christ in our lives. To know that Jesus Christ was characterized by love and yet not to manifest His love is to think little of Jesus Christ. When we see the submission of the Lord Jesus to His Father and then we rebel, we reveal that we do not think much of Jesus Christ. To see the holiness and righteousness of Jesus Christ as He lived before men and then to walk in unholiness and unrighteousness shows that we do not think highly of Jesus Christ. Only when Christ's righteousness is reproduced in our lives can we say that we think well of Jesus Christ.

The important question that John puts forward is not the question, "Can you recognize false doctrine?" His question is, "What do you think of Christ?" What do we think of Him? Do we look at Him through human eyes or through God's eyes? From the human viewpoint He was despised and rejected. Permit the Spirit of God through the Word to reveal the loveliness of the Lord Jesus so that your heart might be drawn to Him and to the Father.

QUESTIONS FOR REFLECTION AND DISCUSSION

Starting Points

1. If you were to list "what's wrong with the world today," what would your top five problems be?

2. When have you seen the power of God break through and overcome something broken or evil?

Exploring the Text

3. What evidence do you see of antichrist influence in religion today? In the political realm? In the social realm? In the moral realm? In the realm of the arts? How can Christians respond?

4. In what ways might Satan make his attacks on the mind in contemporary society? What claims or doubts might he raise?

5. How can the teaching ministry of the Spirit defend against those attacks? When have you experience that defense?

6. In practical terms, what does it mean to be rooted in the Word? How is that a defense against Satan? What steps can you take to stay rooted in the Word?

7. Why is the more important question not, "Can you recognize false doctrine?" but, "What do you think of Christ?" How do our actions show what we think of Christ?

Where Do We Go From Here?

8. How does your life measure up against the "test" John provides in 1 John 2:28–29? Judging by last week only, what would an observer say you think of Christ?

9. Do you need to become more rooted in God's Word? What steps will you take this week?

Lesson: 5

Children of the Father

When our daughter was born, my side of the family was convinced she bore all the features of a Pentecost. My wife's side of the family firmly believed that she looked just like my wife. Both sides claimed to have the photographs to prove it.

God wants His children to "look" just like Him. And the Devil wants his own traits reproduced in his children. Wondering how to tell who belongs to God and who belongs to the Devil? Just look for the family resemblance.

What the Father's Love Is Like
1 John 3:1–3

The theme of chapters one and two in John's first epistle is the absolute holiness of God. As John moves into the next section of his epistle, he concentrates on the fact stated in 1 John 4:8: "God is love." Contemplating the love of God, John seems to be overwhelmed at the enormity of it, as though this were a subject far too big to write about or an idea far too great for the mind to comprehend. He seems to pause as he says, "Behold what manner of love the Father has bestowed on us" (3:1). The word *behold* is like a flashing light on a highway. It is designed to get someone's attention. It calls one to stop, to ponder, to consider a truth that we might too easily pass by.

When John writes to his disciples, he does not focus on the infinity of the love of God, as Paul had done (Eph. 3). John emphasizes the *quality* of God's love. He wants his readers to comprehend how God loves and what He does for those He loves.

First of all, John is emphasizing the *unselfishness* of the love of Cod. Natural love is always selfish love. Human love responds to what is attractive, what will satisfy. That love originates externally in what the other person is like and what he does for the first party. Such love must continually be fed to be sustained and worked at to be maintained.

The love of God originates within Himself, because it is God's nature to love. The love of God does not look at a person and ask, "What can you do for Me?" God sees a person's need and devises ways to meet that need.

The love of God, further, is a *sacrificial* love. This is emphasized in the phrase "bestowed on us" (v. 1). What John has in mind is seen in verse 16 of this chapter when he said, "By this we know love, because He laid down His life for us." The measure of the love of God is that God sacrificed His Son. God sent His Son into this world because He loves the world. Jesus Christ was not sent into the world so much for what He could bring out of this world to the Father, but for what He could bring of the Father into this world. It was sacrificial love that did not count the cost.

John further points out that the love of God is a *separating* love. "Therefore the world does not know us, because it did not know Him" (3:1). Receiving the love of God makes one distinct from the world. The unbeliever may talk about the love of God and the God who is all-loving, but the love of God is known only through the Lord Jesus Christ. The world knows nothing of the love of God in spite of the fact that "God so loved the world that He gave His only begotten Son, that whoever believes in Him should not perish but have everlasting life" (John 3:16).

The world knows of the wrath of God against sin and of the judgment of God against sinners. They recognize the certainty of having to face a just God in a judgment. And when the world sees the believer loved of God and loving God in return, that sends them into a frenzy because they long to be loved. The love of God puts a barrier between the world and the child of God.

In this first verse John also suggests that the love of God is an *enriching* love. A love "that we should be called the children of God." We are born into this world as the children of the evil one (John 8:44). God in His infinite love regenerates those who have been illegitimately born into another family. He gives us a new birth to bring us into His own family. God has given His nature to us by a new birth. God's children are also called "the sons of God," and sonship in Scripture always emphasizes exalted position and rich inheritance.

John also emphasizes that the love of God is a *conforming* love. "We know that when He is revealed, we shall be like Him, for we shall see Him as He is. And everyone who has this hope in Him purifies himself, just as He is pure" (vv. 2–3). God's love causes the believer to become what God wants him to be. God wants believers to be conformed to the image of His Son, and He has destined that one day we shall be like Christ. It is God's purpose that believers begin to be conformed to Christ in this life, and He loves us into that conformity.

The mystery of the love of God is beyond human comprehension. Like Paul, let us pray that we "may be able to comprehend with all the saints what is the width and length and depth and height—to know the love of Christ which passes knowledge" (Eph. 3:18–19)

What Is Sin?
1 John 3:4–6

When a society discusses a moral or ethical issue, it is raising the basic question, "What is sin?" Unfortunately modern society decides such issues by majority vote, so sin is determined by what is acceptable to society.

The apostle John comes to grips with the issue of sin in his epistle: "Whoever commits sin also commits lawlessness, and sin is lawlessness" (3:4). John refers to the Mosaic Law, the absolute standard that was revealed to control the conduct of God's children.

The law was given following God's deliverance of His people out of Egypt. The Israelites had grown up in Egypt and knew nothing of the true and living God. They knew only the gods of Egypt. Their religious life had been molded by Egyptian society. God gave His law to reveal His character to those whom He had redeemed. Israel had believed God and applied the blood of the Passover lamb, but they did not know Him intimately. The law was given to reveal the character of God and the demands that a holy God made on those who would walk in fellowship with Him.

The apostle John recognizes that any failure to obey the revelation of the character of God must be deemed sin. The law says, "God does not; therefore you cannot," and "God does; therefore you must." The law of God is not intended to deprive us of blessing or enjoyment. God gave it to show how He

acts, to reveal who He is, so that we might know
how to act and how to live. One of the simplest tests
as to whether an act is sinful is to ask the question,
"Would the Lord Jesus Christ do that?" Anything
that is unbecoming to the Lord Jesus Christ must be
deemed sinful because it is a violation of the
character of God as revealed in the law of God.

In the New Testament a number of Greek words
are translated by the English word *sin*. Each
communicates a distinct idea about sin. The first
idea is a *failure to attain*, a failure to reach a goal. It
applies to a runner who, after months of
preparation, finds himself in the race and begins to
run well. But as he comes to the end of the race, he
finds his strength waning and he must drop out of
the race.

God's purpose is that His creature be so related to
Him that each finds delight in the other. We were
created to satisfy the heart of God by responding to
the Creator. We are sinners because we have not
reached the purpose that God set before him.

A second word translated *sin* has the idea of
missing the mark, missing the target. This suggests a
soldier who anxiously awaits the approach of the
enemy. As the enemy comes within range, he takes
an arrow from his quiver, carefully fits it to the bow,
and draws back the bowstring. But the arrow veers
off and he misses the mark. Unless an arrow is
perfectly straight, the archer cannot find the mark.
Scripture emphasizes that because of Adam's sin, we
are bent, and we will never find the mark. God's
purpose was to set a straight path for our feet, but
our foot has turned and we do not reach the mark
that God set for us.

A third word translated *sin* has the thought of
failing to measure up to a predetermined standard. A

young man presented himself to an army recruiter. The recruiter filled out all the papers and then sent him to the medical officer. When the officer measured him, he was an inch short of the minimum requirement. The young man had fallen short of the standard. He argued that he was the tallest in his family, but still he was rejected because he did not meet the minimum standard.

That is God's concept of sin. The standard by which God measures a person is not other people. God measures us according to the unalterable perfection of His character and work. God's holiness becomes the measuring rod.

Although we are transgressors, John tells how it is possible for us to fellowship intimately with the Father: "Whoever abides in Him does not sin" (3:6).

When we have our roots down into the Lord Jesus Christ so that His life flows through us, we are so conformed to the standards of God's holiness that we can fellowship with Him. We who become weary in the race can reach the goal. Bent arrows can find God's mark. We who fail to measure up to God's standards can attain the stature of Christ so that God delights in us. The inflexible standards of God are fulfilled as we abide in Jesus Christ.

When John says, "Whoever sins has neither seen Him nor known Him" (3:6), he is not saying that anyone who sins has not been born again, nor that he has lost his salvation. Rather, he affirms that when we sin we have left fellowship with God.

Children of God and Children of the Devil
1 John 3:7–10

Fellowship with God is possible only as we conform to the holiness of God. Jesus Christ came to provide us with a righteousness that would make fellowship with God possible.

In 1 John 3:7 John traces righteousness to its root. Righteous acts come from a righteous nature planted within us, and they are proof of our righteousness. "He who practices righteousness is righteous, just as He [God] is righteous."

The believer possesses two kinds of righteousness. The first is *positional* righteousness in Christ. Paul wrote: "For He has made Him who knew no sin to be sin for us, that we might become the righteousness of God in Him" (2 Cor. 5:21).

Scripture makes it clear that we have no righteousness of our own. "All our righteousnesses are like filthy rags" (Isa. 64:6). "Not by works of righteousness which we have done, but according to His mercy He saved us, through the washing of regeneration and renewing of the Holy Spirit" (Titus 3:5). Jesus Christ, the Righteous One, assumed our guilt to impart His righteousness to us.

The second aspect of righteousness stressed in the Scriptures is *experiential* righteousness, our positional righteousness translated into experience. Paul had this in mind in writing to the Philippians,

> And this I pray, that your love may abound still more and more in knowledge and all discernment, that you may approve the things that are excellent, that you may be sincere and without offense till the day of Christ, being filled with the fruits of righteousness which are by Jesus Christ, to the glory and praise of God. (1:9–11)

John is stressing that righteous acts result from the righteousness of God given to us. Righteousness is the product of the new nature imparted to us by a new birth.

On the other hand, sin is traced to Satan. "He who sins is of the devil, for the devil has sinned from the beginning" (1 John 3:8). Sin begins with Satan and works through fallen human nature. Satan works through the sin nature of a person, whether born again or not, to produce sin.

John now shows us the purpose of the coming of Christ. "For this purpose the Son of God was manifested, that He might destroy the works of the devil" (v. 8). Christ came to provide sinful people with a new nature, enabling us to live holy lives. He came to make it possible for us to fellowship with a holy God.

While some would teach that the new birth eradicates the old sin nature, it is the teaching of Scripture that the sin nature remains with us until we are translated into God's presence. Paul testifies to the existence of the sin nature in the child of God:

> For what I [old nature] am doing, I [new nature] do not understand. For what I [new] will to do, that I [old] do not practice; but what I [new] hate, that I [old] do. If, then, I [old] do what I [new] will not to do, I agree with the law that it is good. But now, it is no longer I [new] who do it, but sin [old] that dwells in me. (Rom. 7:15–17)

Paul is saying that in his experience he recognized two natures operating. The sin nature that he received from his father operated continuously. It was active. It was virulent. Its product was sin. However, Paul recognized that there was a new nature within him imparted by a new birth. This new nature opposed the old, and the product of the new nature was righteousness.

"Whoever has been born of God does not sin" (1 John 3:9). This refers to the new nature imparted to the child of God at his new birth. Peter refers to this new nature: "You may be partakers of the divine nature" (2 Peter 1:4). The nature that God imparts cannot commit sin because it is God's nature.

This is what was in John's mind when he said, "For His seed remains in him." That is, God's seed, God's nature, abides in God's child and that nature cannot sin because it is born of God. John is not saying that sin is impossible in the life of the child of God; He traces sin in the life of the child of God to its root—the old fallen nature. God's children do sin. That is why John wrote, "If we [believers] confess our sins, He is faithful and just to forgive us our sins and to cleanse us from all unrighteousness" (1 John 1:9).

John closes this part of his message by giving us a test of parenthood. "In this the children of God and the children of the devil are manifest: Whoever does not practice righteousness is not of God, nor is he who does not love his brother" (3:10).

There are two tests that one is a child of God. First, you will do righteousness. Unsaved people have no capacity to do righteousness. They may do things that are good in the sight of others, but they cannot act righteously. The only people who can do righteousness acceptable to God are those who have had the righteousness of God imputed to them. Righteousness is God's work in a person. No one can produce righteousness himself. But when God has imputed righteousness to someone, He can then work through that new nature to produce righteousness acceptable to Himself. The first proof that you are a child of God is that the works of God are seen in your life.

The second proof is that the love of God will be produced through God's child. Sinful people are essentially selfish. They cannot love with the unselfish love of God. Unselfish love is proof that God is at work in your life. Love for others becomes a proof of fellowship.

Our fellowship with God, then, does not depend on the eradication of the sin nature. We fellowship with God as we walk in the light of His holiness and as we fellowship one with another.

QUESTIONS FOR REFLECTION AND DISCUSSION

Starting Points
1. Which of your parents' characteristics—physical or otherwise—do people say you have? Which of God's characteristics would you most like to be known for?

2. When did you first become aware of God's love? What response does reflecting on God's marvelous love evoke in you?

Exploring the Text
3. God's love is unselfish, sacrificial, separating, enriching, and conforming. In what ways have you seen these qualities of God's love?

• •

4. How would you describe what it means to be a child of God?

5. "Sin is determined by what is acceptable to society." How do you think contemporary society would define *sin?*

6. How would you define *sin?*

7. Summarize the distinction between positional righteousness and experiential righteousness. What is the relationship of each to salvation? To fellowship with God?

Where Do We Go From Here?

8. Review the two tests of being a child of God that were given at the close of this chapter. List *specific* criteria for each that you can use this week to evaluate how well you are living up to the family name.

9. What benefits do you personally most enjoy as a child of God? Take time to express your praise and gratitude to God, your Father.

Lesson: 6

Siblings Without Rivalry

One of the greatest shocks of parenthood is that the children whom the parent loves so dearly seem so often incapable of getting along with each other. Brothers and sisters fight. And their parents hate it.

God hates it when His children fight, too. Family unity is so important to God that He has made it a household rule: "Love one another."

God's Command to Love
1 John 3:11–15

We tend to believe that in this age of grace there are no commandments for which the child of God is responsible. Nothing could be further from the truth. The commandments of Jesus are as binding on us as the commandments given to Moses in the Old Testament. We are dealing with one of those commandments when John writes, "This is the message that you heard from the beginning, that we should love one another" (1 John 3:11). "Love one another" is not an exhortation; it is a commandment. And the one who does not love as God has loved him is a lawbreaker. No violator of God's commandments can enjoy fellowship with the Father and the Son.

This was not a new commandment John was introducing to his readers. From the opening pages of the Old Testament this commandment had been in force. While some would interpret the phrase "from the beginning" as referring to the beginning of Christ's new revelation while here on earth, it seems best to take this back to the very beginning of divine revelation.

The Pharisees were preoccupied with the Mosaic Law. Realizing that a true Israelite was expected to obey the law, they sought to clarify the law by reducing it to the minimum. They had codified the law into 365 prohibitions and 250 commandments.

However, it became evident to them that it was impossible for anyone to keep all of these, so they tried to arrange the commandments in order of importance. Their inability to conclude which commandment took precedence over the other demonstrates that the law is a unit.

So one of the lawyers of the Pharisees came to Christ to ask a question (Matt. 22:35–40). He was not seeking information; he wanted to embarrass Christ. He asked what seemed to be an unanswerable question. Christ had said that He had come to fulfill the law. If He is to fulfill the law, He must understand the spirit of the law as well as the letter. So the Pharisee asked Jesus, "What is the great commandment in the law? Which commandment takes precedence? Which law is it most important that we observe?"

Without hesitating the Lord answered, "First, love God above all. And second, love your neighbor as yourself."

The law of God was written on two tablets of stone. The first tablet contained commandments that govern our responsibility to God. The second tablet presented commandments and prohibitions that govern our relationship with one another. The only way anyone ever can obey the first part of the law is if love for God takes precedence over all else. When we are totally occupied with God, we will not be occupied with lesser things.

If we are preoccupied with the good of our neighbors we will not do evil to them, so obedience to the second tablet of the law must be founded on love for one's neighbor. Love for one's neighbor is the outgrowth of love for God. Love for God takes precedence over all else and produces love in the family of God; that love extends to those whom God loves. From the beginning, love for God and the consequent love for those who are our neighbors was what God required of us.

Jesus gave the same commandment to the disciples in the Upper Room. "This is My commandment, that you love one another as I have loved you. Greater love has no one than this, than to lay down one's life for his friends. You are My friends if you do whatever I command you" (John 15:12–14). The Lord is emphasizing the connection between love and obedience. Love for God produces obedience. The way to please God is to have a heart that is set on Him. And a heart that is set on Him obeys His commands. Obedience manifests itself when we love others.

A person who knows the command of God but who does not obey is viewed by God as a lawbreaker, and no lawbreaker can have fellowship with a holy God. John, in the verses that immediately preceded, has defined sin as any violation of the law of God. The only way we can enjoy fellowship with the Father is to obey His commandments. And what is on God's list of the greatest commandments? "Love one another."

We are not to love "as Cain who was of the wicked one and murdered his brother. And why did he murder him? Because his works were evil and his brother's righteous" (1 John 3:12). In Genesis 4 we have the record of the birth of two sons to Adam and Eve. Cain, the firstborn, was a farmer. Abel, the second, was a shepherd. Both Cain and Abel received the same revelation about God. When Adam sinned, God became priest, sacrificing an animal and covering Adam's sin with the blood of that animal and covering his nakedness with the skin. That was a revelation on how to approach God.

Later these two brothers offered sacrifices to God. Cain acted in disobedience because of the evil of his heart. Abel acted in obedience because of the righteousness of his heart. When Cain saw that his offering was rejected and his brother's accepted, he murdered his brother. This murder is one of the most heinous crimes recorded in the Word of God. The only crime that could perhaps take precedence was the crime of Judas. Why is this murder such a heinous crime? Because Cain not only killed, he also hated his brother, His sin was a sin against love.

John teaches the importance of obeying the commandment of God, "Love one another," by saying that believers may, like Cain, act on hatred that springs from an evil heart and be guilty of Cain's sin. It was not murder that made Cain's heart evil; the evil produced the murder. Cain's heart was evil because it was not controlled by love. And John is concerned lest an evil heart should manifest itself in the family of God and the family consequently be destroyed.

John recognizes that we will not see this love in the world. Therefore we cannot pattern our conduct after the world, for the world hates. It is only the believer who has the capacity to demonstrate the unselfish love of God, to consider, not himself, but the other person. The love of God is characterized by its pure unselfishness. His love does not consider what the other person can do for the one loving; it is concerned about what the one loving can do for the other person. The world is characterized by hatred, and if we pattern our conduct after the life of the world, we will never enjoy fellowship with the Father and the Son.

John says, "We know that we have passed from death to life, because we love the brethren" (3:14). Love in our hearts for a brother or sister in Christ is evidence that we have been born into God's family, and have been given God's capacity to love, because the world does not have that capacity.

John causes us to examine ourselves when he says, "He who does not love his brother abides in death. Whoever hates his brother is a murderer, and you know that no murderer has eternal life abiding in him" (vv. 14–15). John is not saying that a saved person cannot hate. He is not saying even that a saved person cannot kill, because he can and does. What John is saying is that no one who is controlled by the new life of Christ can hate. No one who is under the control of the love of God can demonstrate hatred in murder. One can be saved and hate, but one cannot be living by the power of the new life of Christ and hate at the same time. We can be alive and still live in the realm of death.

Love always begets obedience. If we are to enter into the fullness of joy, we must love the Father and love the family of God. John has made it very clear that divisions and anger, strife, maliciousness, gossip, and backbiting among believers take one out of the will of God and put him in the class of a lawbreaker. This makes fellowship with God impossible.

Love in Action
1 John 3:16–18

The commandment of God is that the child of God love as God loves. We do not wear the badge of relationship to Jesus Christ until that love is manifested. John now explains the love of God so that his readers can love one another. "By this we know love, because He laid down His life for us" (3:16). In this sacrifice we perceive the love of God.

Frequently in Scripture a writer will refer to one of the saints for the purpose of illustration. When Paul wanted to teach the truth of justification by faith, he appealed to the life of Abraham. As Abraham believed God, so are we to believe God. Many of the Christian virtues can be illustrated by the lives of the saints. But when John would illustrate the love of Christ, he must appeal to God Himself, for the world does not know the love of Christ, nor does it satisfy God's command, "Love one another." So John refers to God the Father.

It was not sufficient for God merely to announce His love to man. It became necessary for God to translate His love into action. The incarnation of Jesus Christ was God veiling the glory of heaven in human flesh and sending His Son into the world. God met humanity's need; the love God reproduced in the child of God responds to the needs of others.

"Whoever has this world's goods, and sees his brother in need, and shuts up his heart from him, how does the love of God abide in him?" (v. 17) is an interpretation and application of verse 16. God in His wisdom met for human need by offering salvation. John wants us to realize that the love of God reproduced in us will recognize the need and meet the needs of others. The love of God is not only an emotional response such as mercy or pity. The love of God will give rise to such emotions, but we have not loved with the love of God until we act.

We ask, "But whom am I to love?" John is writing about love in the family of God. We are responsible to love the members of the family of God—the family of God with whom we are closely associated. But if we stop here we are little better than the lawyer who came to test Christ. He was a scholar of Mosaic Law and its interpretation. He tested Jesus by asking, "What laws must I keep to have eternal life?" Our Lord responded, "What is written in the law?" The lawyer replied, using the same response the Lord had given when He was asked this question on another occasion. The lawyer said, "You shall love the LORD your God with all your heart, with all your soul, with all your strength, and with all your mind, and your neighbor as yourself" (Luke 10:27). Love for God means total commitment to God and love for one's neighbor demands obedience to the law of God in fulfilling every social relationship. So love is the fulfillment of the law.

After the lawyer summarized the law he stood convicted of his own unworthiness. His excuse was to plead ignorance. He asked, "And who is my neighbor?"

Jesus then told the familiar story of the man traveling down from Jerusalem to Jericho. As he was going through the wilderness of Judea among mountain recesses, he was attacked by thieves. The thieves stripped him and wounded him. He was lying alongside the road, obviously in need. A priest walked by, and he recognized the man's need. The priest had the means to meet that need, but he had no compassion. A little later a Levite passed by. He recognized the need and could have met the man's need. But he too had no compassion.

Later a Samaritan, despised by the Jews, came by. He responded to the need. First he bound up the man's wounds, using oil to soothe and wine to purify. He brought the man to an inn and cared for him. He even provided for the man's future needs.

The Lord asked the lawyer, "Which of these three do you think was neighbor to the man?" And the lawyer answered, "The one that showed mercy to him." So our Lord's definition of our neighbor is, "Anyone in need, whose need you are able to meet."

To know the need but have no capacity to meet it does not put me under obligation. Nor am I responsible if I am ignorant of the need. But where there is knowledge coupled with ability, I have a responsibility to demonstrate the love of Christ to one in need.

This is a very pointed lesson; it removes the boundaries from our narrow concepts of our responsibility. Our responsibility becomes as wide as the love of God.

John gives a word of caution: our affection must not be in words alone, words must be accompanied by deeds. He does not say, "Don't tell anybody you love them." He says, "Don't let words be your only communication."

People are often surprised by the love shown to them by members of their church. But isn't it unfortunate that someone has to be helpless or in desperate need before we show affection? To smother love or to leave it unexpressed is to frustrate the work of the Spirit. We must learn to express our love for one another. Love does not ask, "What can you do for me?" Love asks, "What can I do for you?"

Love asks not so much, "How are you today?" but "What can I do for you today?"

Whom am I responsible to love? Anyone in need. There is not one of us who does not need to be loved. We have the responsibility to show the love of Christ by meeting one another's need.

Coming Full Circle
1 John 3:19–24

Because we love God, we are commanded to love one another. But in loving one another, we find our faith confirmed, our relationship with God assured, and our worship and prayer life made more effective. When we work toward fellowship with other believers, we gain fellowship with God.

John tells us that a believer's love for others is confirmation of sound doctrine. "And by this we know that we are of the truth, and shall assure our hearts before Him" (v. 19). The apostles wanted believers to stand firm in the truth. The body of truth revealed to the apostles by the Spirit was called "The Faith" or "The Truth."

False doctrine will show itself in evil practice, but true doctrine will produce obedience to God's commands. If you examine a bush in your yard and find a tender green bud, you know it has survived the winter. The roots must be alive for a bud to appear. In the same way, love for others reveals that we hold to sound doctrine.

Love for one another also assures us of our relationship to the Father. John deals with the negative aspect first. "If our heart condemns us, God is greater than our heart, and knows all things" (v. 20). John recognizes that believers will have to say, "I know I do not love as Christ loved." The love of

Christ does show itself in us, but that is not our outstanding characteristic. If I gauge my relationship to the Father by emotions and experience, I would have no assurance of my relationship to God. While we judge our relationship to God by experience, John instructs us to determine this relationship by faith. God knows that we have faith in Him. If our hearts condemn us and question whether we are related to Jesus Christ, God is satisfied because He judges on the basis of faith.

There is, tragically, a theological wave engulfing the church that determines doctrine, not by the Word of God, but by personal experience. When confronted with the Word of God, multitudes say, "I don't care what the Bible says, my experience tells me different." They are basing their relationship to God on sinful human experience, and consequently they are insecure.

John says, "Beloved, if our heart does not condemn us, we have confidence toward God" (v. 21). If our heart does not convict us of breaking God's love commandment, this means we are in fact loving others, and this assures us.

John explains that obedience to Christ's love commandment is the basis for answered prayer. "Whatever we ask we receive from Him, because we keep His commandments and do those things that are pleasing in His sight" (v. 22). Loving one another is a prerequisite to answered prayer. We have the right to pray because we are related to Jesus Christ by faith, but that relationship does not guarantee that our prayers will be answered.

Not until we have obeyed Christ's commandment will our prayers be answered. On the other hand, if we do not keep His commandments our prayers will not be answered.

John tells us there are two commandments. First, "Believe on the name of His Son Jesus Christ" (v. 23). Faith in Jesus Christ establishes relationship with the Father and is the foundation of prayer. The second commandment is as essential as the first: "Love one another, as He gave us commandment." If a child of God is out of fellowship with another believer, he is out of fellowship with the Father. When the right relationship does not exist between children in a family, the relationship between the father and children will also be strained. Prayer will be hindered if family members are out of fellowship.

The command to love is as much an imperative as the command to believe. The necessity of faith is obvious. The necessity to love ought to be equally obvious. The Lord made this clear in Matthew 5. He is speaking to Jews, who worshiped and prayed in a form that differs from ours, but the lesson is pertinent nonetheless. "If you bring your gift to the altar, and there remember that your brother has something against you, leave your gift there before the altar, and go your way. First be reconciled to your brother, and then come and offer your gift" (Matt. 5:23–24). Jesus says that the door to God can be closed, not because God is not gracious nor because He cannot hear, but because we are alienated from our brothers and sisters in Christ.

As important as it is for you to worship and pray, it is more important to be reconciled with your brother. Do not go to God until you have straightened out matters with your brother. What could be clearer? Disruption of fellowship with a brother, for any cause, disrupts fellowship with God. We are related to Jesus Christ by faith when we obey the first commandment, and we are able to pray to God when we have obeyed the second. Love is the basis of answered prayer.

Finally, John points out again that obedience to this commandment to love as Christ loved is the basis of our fellowship with the Father. "Now he who keeps His commandments abides in Him" (1 John 3:24). John has told us he was writing to introduce his readers to the glorious truth of fellowship with the Father and with His Son (1:3). There is no real satisfaction for the child of God apart from intimate fellowship with the Father. "And these things we write to you that your joy may be full" (1:4). But there can be no fellowship with the Father apart from fellowship with the saints. The believer who keeps God's commandments of faith in God and love for one another abides in fellowship with Him.

QUESTIONS FOR REFLECTION AND DISCUSSION

Starting Points

1. When you were growing up, what was your relationship like with your sibling(s)? Why do you think kids fight so much?

2. How would you characterize the "sibling" relationships in your congregation or denomination? In the church worldwide? Why do you think Christians fight so much?

Exploring the Text

3. How is love for brothers and sisters in Christ an evidence of salvation?

4. What is the relationship between hate and salvation? Between hate and fellowship with God?

5. "Where there is knowledge coupled with ability, I have a responsibility to demonstrate the love of Christ to one in need" (p. 88). Give some specific examples of situations in which one would be called to love in action. What form might that demonstration of love take?

6. How well does your church support those in crisis? How well does your church express love when there is no crisis? What are some appropriate ways to express love to other believers?

7. What is the connection between our relationships with other believers and worship or prayer?

Where Do We Go From Here?

8. Do you need to be reconciled with a brother or sister in Christ? What can you do to repair that relationship?

9. To whom can you show love as a brother or sister in Christ this week? What will you do?

Lesson: 7

Clearly Counterfeit

A young federal agent was assigned to a department responsible to identify and track down counterfeit money. Eager to be effective in his work, the agent diligently studied each new counterfeit bill, memorizing the exact flaws that had marked it as a phony. But as the weeks passed, instead of becoming more confident, he grew increasingly frustrated. Every time he thought he knew what flaws to look for, a new bill, with different deviations, came across his desk. Finally an older and wiser colleague said to him, "Don't study the phonies. Study the real thing. Anything that doesn't match up is a fake."

Our world is flooded with spiritual counterfeits. To become familiar with all of them would be an overwhelming task. But fortunately, it's an unnecessary task. To avoid being taken in, all we really need to know is what the real thing looks like. Anything that doesn't match up is a fake.

Testing the Teacher
1 John 4:1–6

John speaks urgently of loving one another. But he also wants to safeguard God's children against prostituting their affections. An indiscriminate love will violate the commandment to love as Christ loved. Therefore John writes, "Beloved, do not believe every spirit, but test the spirits, whether they are of God; because many false prophets are gone out into the world" (4:1).

The spirits John wants his readers to test are not beings that come from the demonic world. He is referring to teachers or prophets.

To understand John's concern, we need to know a little about the preaching arrangement in the early church. First-century believers knew little of a formal arrangement where the assembly of believers had a pastor who taught the Word of God. Like apostles, the teachers traveled from church to church. They depended on hospitality when they came to teach.

We read in Hebrews 13:1–2, "Let brotherly love continue. Do not forget to entertain strangers, for by so doing some have unwittingly entertained angels [God's emissaries]." The obligation to love included extending hospitality, particularly to those whom God had sent to minister the Word of God.

We can well imagine a knock on the door and the householder opening the door to a man who would identify himself as one sent by God with His message. The householder would remember John's command to show hospitality as a sign of love, and so he would be likely to invite the visitor in. But John cautioned that there are both true and false teachers. Believers must discriminate between the two. John gives this warning to safeguard the commandment to love one another. One must use discrimination in his affection.

John begins by pointing out that there are two kinds of teachers: those who come with the truth and those who deny the truth and come with error.

As he writes further, John draws a distinction between the origin of the false teachers and the origin of the true teachers. In verse 3 he says,

> Every spirit that does not confess that Jesus Christ has come in the flesh is not of God. And this is the spirit of the Antichrist, which you have heard was coming, and is now already in the world.

Again in verse 5, "They are of the world. Therefore they speak as of the world, and the world hears them." The false teachers originate from the world.

Earlier in the study of this epistle we have seen that *the world* is an organized system under the headship of Satan. In order to attain his goal of dethroning God and enthroning himself, Satan sends out representatives to teach. They teach the thinking of this world, the thinking of Satan, and they get a response because they are saying what the worldling wants to hear.

In contrast there are those who are of God. "We are of God. He who knows God hears us; he who is not of God does not hear us. By this we know the spirit of truth and the spirit of error" (v. 6).

The true teacher comes by divine authority. His authority is in the truth, and the Spirit of God testifies to the truth. When the emissary of God speaks to God's children, the Spirit of God confirms the truth to the listeners.

John now considers the two doctrines put forward by these two teachers. First he deals with the true doctrine. "By this you know the Spirit of God: Every spirit that confesses that Jesus Christ has come in the flesh is of God" (4:2). The Word of God is the test of the doctrine of any teacher.

● ●

This is clearly illustrated in the Old Testament when, after God had revealed the law through Moses, He explains how to detect a false prophet:

> If there arises among you a prophet or a dreamer of dreams, and he gives you a sign or a wonder, and the sign or the wonder comes to pass, of which he spoke to you, saying, "Let us go after other gods"—which you have not known— "and let us serve them," you shall not listen to the words of that prophet or that dreamer of dreams. (Deut. 13:1–3)

Here is a prophet who appears before the people of God claiming to be God's spokesman. He performs miracles and predicts the future. Looking at his prediction and at the wonders that he did, one would say, "This man must come by the power of God. We must listen to what he says." But in spite of the signs, and visions, and predictions, God demands:

> You shall not listen to the words of that prophet or that dreamer of dreams, for the LORD your God is testing you to know whether you love the LORD your God with all your heart and with all your soul. You shall walk after the LORD your God and fear Him, and keep His commandments and obey His voice; you shall serve Him and hold fast to Him. But that prophet or that dreamer of dreams shall be put to death, because he has spoken in order to turn you away from the LORD your God, who brought you out of the land of Egypt and redeemed you from the house of bondage, to entice you from the way in which the LORD your God commanded you to walk. So you shall put away the evil from your midst. (Deut. 13:3–5)

Such a man may seem to have the credentials to prove that he has come from God, but if that prophet's word was contrary to the Word of God, he was to be put to death. The evidence that a prophet is a true prophet lies in the word that he speaks. Does it conform to the Word of God? If it does not, he is a false prophet.

God is zealous to preserve His Word because it is our access to Him. When a false prophet changes that Word, he has closed the door that God has opened.

Jesus warned his disciples that they would need discernment to identify false teachers coming in the guise of God's messengers:

> Beware of false prophets, who come to you in sheep's clothing, but inwardly they are ravenous wolves. You will know them by their fruits. Do men gather grapes from thornbushes or figs from thistles? Even so, every good tree bears good fruit, but a bad tree bears bad fruit. A good tree cannot bear bad fruit, nor can a bad tree bear good fruit. Every tree that does not bear good fruit is cut down and thrown into the fire. Therefore by their fruits you will know them. (Matt. 7:15–20)

Paul had given a similar warning to the Ephesian church—probably the very church to whom John wrote his first epistle—when he wrote,

> Therefore take heed to yourselves and to all the flock, among which the Holy Spirit has made you overseers, to shepherd the church of God which He purchased with His own blood. For I know this, that after my departure savage wolves will come in among you, not sparing the flock. Also from among yourselves men will rise up, speaking perverse things, to draw away the disciples after themselves. (Acts 20:28–30)

John gives us a specific test by which we determine whether someone is a true teacher or a counterfeiter. He tells us the one mark of authenticity that every teacher must match up against: "Every spirit that confesses that Jesus Christ has come in the flesh is of God" (1 John 4:2).

In the first chapter of his gospel John outlined the doctrine of the person of Christ: Christ is the eternal Son of the eternal God; He is equal with God; He is the Creator; He is the One who reveals the Father to us; He is life; He is the Savior. Now John can write and say, "The test of any teacher is what he thinks about the person of Jesus Christ." If a man denies the truth about the person of Jesus Christ, he is a false teacher. He does not come from God. He is an emissary of Satan, no matter how much he professes to be God's spokesman. Without exception, false teachers deny that Jesus Christ is the eternal Son of the eternal God, who by His substitutionary death on the cross provided us with eternal salvation.

In his second letter, John writes, "If anyone comes to you and does not bring this doctrine, do not receive him into your house nor greet him" (2 John 10). If we extend hospitality without distinguishing between God's messengers and Satan's messengers, we are violating the principle of love. If one professes to come with God's message, and, without testing him, we expose the saints to his false teaching, we are his partner in deception. And if we send him on his way with our blessing (that is, material support), then we are convicted by the Word: "for he who greets him shares in his evil deeds" (2 John 11).

John's warning does not come with a knell of doom, however, but with encouragement: "You are of God, little children, and have overcome them, because He who is in you is greater than he who is in the world" (1 John 4:4). Even the "littlest child" in faith can have confidence when testing the spirits, because of the indwelling of the Holy Spirit. In 1 John 2:20 we read, "You have an anointing from the Holy One, and you know all things." The child of God who listens with the ear of the Spirit of God will not be deceived by error, because the Spirit will never approve the deception of a false teacher.

In fact, the Ephesian church had overcome many false teachers, as John testified in recording Christ's letter to that church: "I know your works, your labor, your patience, and that you cannot bear those who are evil. And you have tested those who say they are apostles and are not, and have found them liars" (Rev. 2:2). So John truly could say, "You have overcome them."

In the apostle's day the Word had to be communicated person-to-person. With the many means of communication today, we can invite all kinds of false teachers into our homes without being in the presence of another person. Whether a teacher comes in person to propagate his doctrine, or whether he does it by some other means, if we invite him into our home we have become a partaker of his evil deeds.

We have no right to accept any word that purports to come from God without testing it by the Word of God. God commands us to love. But he safeguards that by commanding us to be discriminating in our love. Test the teachers by the Word of God. Test them by their doctrine of the person and the work of Jesus Christ, for multitudes of false teachers have come to propagate Satan's doctrine. We must test the spirits, lest we fall into the deception of the evil one. But we can test them without fear, because He who is in us is greater than he who is in the world.

• •

QUESTIONS FOR REFLECTION AND DISCUSSION

Starting Points

1. Can you recall a time when you were completely taken in—by a sales pitch, a practical joke, or some other deception? Why do you think you fell for the lie?

2. How vulnerable do you feel to spiritual counterfeits?

Exploring the Text

3. Imagine you were writing to warn a new Christian not to be deceived by phony teachings and philosophies. As clearly and concisely as you can, what test would you offer to distinguish between truth and falsehood?

4. Do you have any experience with cults, or know anyone who does? Why do you think many cults are so successful at attracting people?

5. Besides cults and other obvious religious messages, what other "false teachers" do you encounter in today's society?

6. How do these false teachers enter your home? How do you respond to them?

Where Do We Go From Here?

8. In what ways have you been "offering hospitality" to false teachers? What will you do about it?

9. Do you know someone who may be vulnerable to deception—perhaps someone who is young in the faith or young in years? How can you encourage and enable that person to become well-versed enough in the truth to be able to identify falsehood?

Lesson: 8

The Heartbeat of God

The love of God in Christ had so captivated the apostle John that it became the central theme of his ministry. The critic sees this note woven like a golden thread throughout 1 John and concludes that it is the rambling of a senile mind. But how the heart of the child of God leaps in response to the love that John showed for the Lord and for the saints. Far from being the musings of a senile man, this epistle throbs with the heartbeat of God.

God Sent His Son
1 John 4:7–11

God demonstrated His love by sending Christ: "In this the love of God was manifested toward us, that God has sent His only begotten Son into the world" (1 John 4:9). God clothed Himself with flesh and stepped out of heaven into this world and lived a life so that we could become intimately knowledgeable about God. God did not have to come into this world to reveal Himself. But He chose to do so. Why? Because God is love. God wanted to reveal Himself and His love toward those who were separated from Him.

God also manifested His love through the death of His Son. God's love for the Son is eternal and unchangeable, but God gave His Son up to death.

The measure of the love of God is not so much a measure of the distance from heaven to earth as it is a measure of the distance from the throne to the cross, for it is there that we see the greatness of the love of God.

When the Son of God came into the world, there was no separation between the Father and the Son, for they continued to enjoy intimate communion. But when the Son went to the cross, He was separated from the Father by death. And in that separation we have a revelation of the love of God.

The apostle tells us that the Son came into the world "that we might live through Him" (v. 9). God gives of Himself to those who put their faith in Jesus Christ and put themselves under His atoning death. God takes those who were enemies and dead in sin, and gives them life and brings them into His own family as His well-beloved children.

The world stands in amazement when a family takes a retarded or deformed child into their home and loves the child as if he or she were their own. How much greater was the love of God that looked on us in our deformity of sin and took us into His family and made us His heirs.

To climax this survey of the love of God, the apostle says, "In this is love, not that we loved God, but that He loved us and sent his Son to be the propitiation for our sins" (v. 10). John is referring to the value of the death of Christ and the great work that God accomplished for sinners on the cross so that we might become members of God's family. *Propitiation* is one of the most beautiful words in the Word of God. In Leviticus 16 we find in one of Israel's annual rituals a foreshadowing of Christ as our propitiation. There Moses instructed Israel concerning the Day of Atonement. That day begins with the recognition that all people are separated from God and have in themselves no approach to God. God took up residence between the cherubim above the mercy seat on the ark of the covenant. Not even Aaron could come into the presence of God on his own merit. Aaron was commanded to kill a goat, which provided access into the presence of God. The blood of the sacrifice was to be placed on the mercy seat.

The writer to the Hebrews shows that Jesus Christ has fulfilled this Old Testament ritual. The New Testament writers tell us that because of sin we cannot approach God. But Jesus Christ has come and taken our sins in His own body. He has covered those sins with His own blood and offered Himself as a sacrifice to God. "How much more shall the blood of Christ, who through the eternal Spirit offered Himself without spot to God, cleanse your conscience from dead works to serve the living God?" (9:14).

Jesus Christ is the One who satisfies God. The blood of Christ is the basis on which God is satisfied; so God can now stretch out His hands to sinners. The death of Jesus Christ did not change the heart of God, as if One who hated us now loves us; rather it opened the floodgate so that the love of God for sinners could be poured out to us through Jesus Christ. This is what John has in mind when he speaks of *propitiation.*

Love for God never originates in the heart of man. Love originates in the heart of God and kindles a love for God in the heart of God' s enemies. That is what John is emphasizing when he says, "Not that we loved God." God's love for sinners brings us into the full experience of His love and into full partnership in His life.

• •

"Let us love one another" (vv. 7, 11) emphasizes an added facet of the truth John taught earlier. In chapter 3, love for the brethren referred to physical and material needs. Now John presents an entirely different concept—spiritual needs. We ought to share spiritual blessings with others to bring them into the love of Christ and the life of Christ.

This was the nature of Christ's ministry. He continually was meeting the physical needs of men. He fed the hungry. He healed the sick. He raised the dead. But our Lord was far more involved in meeting spiritual needs.

Our Lord chose a few men. He could have ministered to multiplied thousands every time He chose to teach. But our Lord left the multitudes and withdrew to minister to a handful of men. Scripture does not belabor what He did for them physically, nor how He provided for them materially. But it does tell us how He invested His life in these men and taught them the truth of God, and revealed the love of God, and prepared them for a ministry of the Word of God.

Christ was in the business of making disciples. He made disciples by dealing with men individually. John is eager that his children, who have recognized an obligation to minister to one another materially, should occupy themselves in a spiritual ministry to one another. He desired that each saint seek out another individual with whom to share the love of Christ and the life of Christ and build into the life of that individual what Christ had built into them. Christ made disciples. Now John wants his spiritual children to make disciples.

We measure our ministry by the number to whom we minister. A Sunday school teacher counts the size of her class. The pastor pays attention to the size of the congregation. God does not evaluate by numbers, but by results. Results do not necessarily come by ministering to multitudes, but by building into the life of the individual.

In our relationships we begin with friendship. People become friends because of some mutual interest such as a hobby or business. And then friendship ought to progress to fellowship, which is friendship that takes on the added dimension of the Lord Jesus Christ. Fellowship, in turn, lays the foundation for discipleship, which is the process of helping a fellow believer to mature in Christ. A congregation may *mature* by sitting together under the ministry of the Word of God, but a congregation will *multiply* when each individual disciples another.

If you have thought you discharged your responsibility to the obligation of love by looking after the material needs of some saint, then let God open your vision to another concern: to share the love of Christ and the life of Christ by making a disciple for the Lord Jesus. The love of God demands it, and we do not fulfill our obligation to His love until we do it.

The Savior of the World
1 John 4:12–15

God's love is a selfless love. It considers only the welfare of those whom He loves. If God considered Himself, He would not have sent the Lord Jesus Christ into the world.

Why should an innocent man die? The apostle John gives us the answer. "And we have seen and testify that the Father has sent the Son as the Savior of the world" (v. 14). There is perhaps no more tender name given to Jesus than *Savior*. He is the

Lord Jesus Christ. He is the Son of God. He is the Son of Man. He is the Servant of Jehovah. He is David's greater Son. But above all, He is the Savior.

The Word of God clearly reveals to us the slavery from which we have been delivered by our Savior. First of all, because we were sinners, we were enslaved to Satan. We needed to be delivered from Satan's dominion. When Adam disobeyed God, he consciously submitted to the authority of Satan. He became a slave of Satan. We had no power to loose the shackles of Satan and deliver ourselves. And this necessitated a Deliverer who could reach us in our slavery to Satan and proclaim liberty to the captives.

Paul writes: "He has delivered us from the power of darkness and conveyed us into the kingdom of the Son of His love" (Col. 1:13). God has delivered us from the rule of Satan and brought us into His kingdom, where He rules as Sovereign.

The Lord Jesus also came to save us from slavery to the law. The law was a taskmaster, a ruler over slaves. The law passed judgment on all who violated the holy standards of God revealed in the law. Paul writes that Jesus Christ blotted out the handwriting of the indictment against us. "He has taken it out of the way, having nailed it to the cross. Having disarmed principalities and powers, He made a public spectacle of them, triumphing over them in it" (Col. 2:14–15). By His death Christ satisfied the demands of the law so that we might be set free.

We were also enslaved to sin. We had no love for God, no desire to do the will of God. We loved sin, and we obeyed its pull. All that human nature produced was sin in the sight of God—totally unacceptable to Him. God saw that the heart of man was "only evil continually" (Gen. 6:5).

In Colossians 1:14, following his declaration that we have been delivered from the power of Satan, Paul declares that Christ is He "in whom we have redemption through His blood, the forgiveness of sins." The word *forgive* means to put away, to separate the sinner from the sins so that we bear them no longer. Not only has God lifted the burden of sin, but He also has taken us from the mastery of sin, so that we might serve a new master.

Christ also came to be Savior from the realm of death. There are two aspects of death as the penalty for sin. When God said to Adam, "In the day that you eat of it, you shall surely die" (Gen. 2:17), God was speaking primarily of spiritual death. Spiritual death is the separation of the soul from God. Had Adam not sinned, had he continued in his intimate fellowship with God, he would have lived forever. The seeds of corruption were not in his body at Creation, but the moment Adam disobeyed God spiritual death fell upon him. Adam was separated from God by a great gulf that he could not cross. The result of spiritual death was physical death. It came as the penalty for Adam's separation from God.

The apostle Paul makes it clear that Christ came to save the world from slavery to death. Paul writes, "For the wages of sin is death; but the gift of God is eternal life in Christ Jesus our Lord" (Rom. 6:23). Eternal life is the life of God imparted to the one who trusts Christ as Savior.

Jesus Christ came into the realm of spiritual death. He was separated from God, when He cried on the cross, "My God, my God, why have You forsaken Me?" By that cry He testified that He left the realm of life and entered the realm of spiritual death so that we might pass from death into life through Him.

John also writes that Christ lifts us out of physical death into the newness of life.

> Most assuredly, I say to you, he who hears My word and believes in Him who sent Me has everlasting life, and shall not come into judgment, but has passed from death into life. Most assuredly, I say to you, the hour is coming, and now is, when the dead will hear the voice of the Son of God; and those who hear will live. For as the Father has life in Himself, so He has granted the Son to have life in Himself, and has given Him authority to execute judgment also, because He is the Son of Man. Do not marvel at this; for the hour is coming in which all who are in the graves will hear His voice and come forth—those who have done good, to the resurrection of life, and those who have done evil, to the resurrection of condemnation. (John 5:24–29)

The unsaved person lives with an uncontrollable fear of death because of the conviction that after death is the judgment. No one is prepared to stand alone before a holy and righteous Judge. But Jesus Christ is the Savior, not only from death, but also from the fear of death. For the child of God has the assurance given to us in 2 Corinthians 5:8 that to be absent from the body is to be present with the Lord. We face no long journey, no dark valley, no time interval. We are immediately transformed out of this life into the presence of the Lord Jesus Christ. This hope is the result of God giving His Son to be our Savior.

Love Perfected
1 John 4:16–21

In chapters 3 and 4 of this epistle John has been appealing to the hearts of believers by emphasizing one command, "Love one another." As John concludes this segment of his letter, he is speaking of the perfection of love. God, who has begun a process, is concerned with its conclusion. He wants to bring us to conformity to Jesus Christ. So John writes, "He who abides in love abides in God, and God in him" (4:16).

The word *abide* is one of John's favorites. He has used it throughout this epistle. To abide in God is to have one's spiritual roots so deeply implanted in Him that His life flows through the total person and shows itself in that person's life. The plant sends roots into the soil, drawing moisture and nutrients that supply life. In the same way, when one is abiding in the love of God this love will permeate the person's personality so that he will live a different life. People will see the love of God in him.

John speaks of love made perfect in verse 17. God's intention when He gave His love to us was to make us perfect. Paul states in Romans 8:29 that it is God's plan that we might be conformed to the image of His Son. God wants to reproduce Jesus Christ in His children so that, when a nonbeliever looks at the child of God, he will come to know the Father.

The presence of this love in the child of God gives us boldness to approach the Father. Our love is made perfect "that we may have boldness in the day of judgment; because as He is, so are we in this world" (1 John 4:17). This boldness is the freedom to come into the presence of God. This is the freedom Adam had before the Fall. God and Adam enjoyed intimate fellowship in the Garden, but Adam lost his freedom when he sinned. How can we who are sinners by nature and by choice be free to come into the presence of the holy God who condemns sin? It is because we have been made like Jesus.

In Jesus Christ we stand as those who are righteous in the sight of God. That glorious fact gives us boldness. We have freedom to come into the presence of God. That is why the writer to the Hebrews can say, "Let us therefore come boldly to the throne of grace, that we may obtain mercy and find grace to help in time of need" (4:16). We do not crawl into the presence of God; we come before Him with the full confidence that we have been accepted in Christ. We know that "there is therefore now no condemnation to those who are in Christ Jesus" (Rom. 8:1).

The one in whom love is perfected also lives without fear. "There is no fear in love; but perfect love casts out fear" (1 John 4:18). The word *fear* in the Bible is used in two different senses. The first usage refers to reverence, or awe and respect. The child of God never loses his reverence for God, his sense of unworthiness as he approaches the glory of God. And it is right that we should fear God, but this is not what John is talking about when he says there is no fear in love.

John uses the word to denote dread or terror. When John says we have no fear, he means that Christ's love casts out our dread of God. Respect for God produces a godly awe, but sin produces fear.

John has commanded us over and over again to love one another; to love God; to love the family of God. To safeguard against the misconception that we originate this love, John writes, "We love Him because He first loved us." The love that perfects us and the love that gives us boldness and the love that removes fear does not originate with us; it originates with God. Any affection that we offer to God did not originate in our hearts, because we naturally hate God. But when God showers His love on us, that cold heart of stone is transformed so that it responds to the love of God.

In commanding us to "love one another," John is not saying that believers must generate this love in their own hearts. He is saying, rather, that if we open our hearts to the love of God, God's love will produce love for God and love for the family of God. John can command us to love, but we cannot do it. God, however, can flood our hearts with His love so that we love.

John concludes by assuring us that the love of God will show itself in love for one another:

> If someone says, "I love God," and hates his brother, he is a liar; for he who does not love his brother whom he has seen, how can he love God whom he has not seen? And this commandment we have from Him: that he who loves God must love his brother also. (vv. 20–21)

The apostle Paul tells of his persuasion that

> neither death nor life, nor angels nor principalities nor powers, nor things present nor things to come, nor height nor depth, nor any other created thing, shall be able to separate us from the love of God which is in Christ Jesus our Lord. (Rom 8:38–39)

We cannot be separated from God, and that love is to so permeate our beings that it shows itself not only in loving God but also in becoming a channel through which God loves others.

• •

QUESTIONS FOR REFLECTION AND DISCUSSION

Starting Points

1. Think of a time when someone made you feel truly loved. What did that person do? What was the effect on you?

2. What has God done to make you feel truly loved? What impact has it had on you?

Exploring the Text

3. In concrete terms, what does it mean to make a disciple? How does that fulfill the command to "love one another"? In what other ways can believers meet one another's spiritual needs?

4. How does one go about making someone a disciple? Are you discipling someone? If not, should you be?

5. Reflect on those things from which our Savior set us free: slavery to Satan, the law, sin, and death. Write a psalm or prayer expressing your response to Christ.

6. In what way does love cast out fear? How do you experience that truth?

7. How does knowing that love originates with God and not with us affect your understanding of the command to love?

Where Do We Go From Here?

8. Assess how well you are obeying the command to help meet others' spiritual needs. What further actions might you take?

9. Over the course of this week set aside time to reflect on the different areas in which Christ has set you free. Respond to each by journaling, spending time in specific worship and prayer, or in some other way responding to your Savior.

Lesson: 9

Winners and Witnesses

"In the fight between you and the world, back the world," Frank Zappa is supposed to have said.

He was wrong, of course.

Because the fight between us and the world isn't fought with fists, it's fought with faith. And faith overcomes the world.

Overcoming the World
1 John 5:1–5

Many of the decisions we make have a major effect on our life: the schools we attend, the person we marry, the profession we follow, the position we accept. But no decision has such widespread influence for time and eternity as the decision we make about Jesus Christ.

John speaks of this decision and the new birth that results as he opens chapter 5. "Whoever believes that Jesus is the Christ is born of God."

The term *Christ* or *Messiah* embodies much biblical truth. It brings to our attention both the person and the work of the Lord Jesus Christ. According to the Old Testament, the One who came to be the Messiah would not only be the Son of David, but He would also be the Son of God. During the course of His earthly life, Jesus Christ laid less claim to being Mary's son, and He placed more

• •

emphasis on being the Son of God. Man could not redeem man; only God could do that.

After offering Himself to Israel as the Messiah, Christ authenticated His person by the many miracles He performed. As the disciples saw the wonders and signs that came from His hands, they were led to the conviction that this One was the Son of God. They believed on Him (Matt. 16:16). Salvation depends on accepting the person of Jesus Christ, consenting to the biblical truth that He is the Son of God. Faith itself does not save; it is a Person, the Savior, who saves.

The term *Messiah* also brings to our attention the work of Christ. God made it clear in the Old Testament that without the shedding of blood there is no remission of sin. The Messiah is described in Isaiah:

> He was wounded for our transgressions, He was bruised for our iniquities; the chastisement for our peace was upon Him, and by His stripes we are healed. All we like sheep have gone astray; we have turned, every one, to his own way; and the LORD has laid on Him the iniquity of us all. (Isa. 53:5–6)

The Messiah must become the sin-bearer in death. One who comes to Christ not only trusts Him as a Person, but he also trusts His work at Calvary. There sinless blood was shed to provide a covering for the sins of the world. We must trust in this work of Christ.

John says that whoever believes that Jesus is the Christ, or Messiah, is "born of God" (1 John 5:1). John next presents three evidences of the new birth.

"Everyone who loves Him who begot also loves him who is begotten of Him" (v. 1). This is the summary of what John has presented in chapters 3 and 4 so emphatically. God has commanded those who love Him to demonstrate this love by loving those whom He loves. Love for the brethren becomes the first evidence of the new birth.

Love cannot originate in the heart of a natural man because he is selfish and his love is directed inward. When one can go beyond the bounds of natural love and manifest the love of God, when one can love unselfishly, this is evidence of being born into the family of God.

After a worship service in Africa in which I had the privilege of taking part, one of the missionaries handed me a poem entitled "Perfect Love," written by an anonymous writer. In a simple and practical style these lines describe our love for fellow believers.

> Slow to suspect,
>   Quick to trust.
> Slow to condemn,
>   Quick to justify.
> Slow to offend,
>   Quick to defend.
> Slow to expose,
>   Quick to shield.
> Slow to reprimand,
>   Quick to forebear.
> Slow to belittle,
>   Quick to appreciate.
> Slow to demand,
>   Quick to give.
> Slow to hinder,
>   Quick to help.
> Slow to provoke,
>   Quick to conciliate.
> Slow to resent,
>   Quick to forgive.

In verses 2 and 3, John presents a second evidence of the new birth. "By this we know that we love the children of God, when we love God and keep His commandments. For this is the love of God, that we keep His commandments. And his commandments are not burdensome." The second proof of the new birth is obedience to the Word of God. The Lord said,

> If anyone loves Me, he will keep My word; and My Father will love him, and We will come to him and make Our home with him. He who does not love Me does not keep My words; and the word which you hear is not Mine but the Father's who sent Me. (John 14:23–24)

Or again in John 15:10, "If you keep My commandments, you will abide in My love."

There in the Upper Room Jesus impressed on the disciples that God expected implicit obedience to His Word as an evidence of their love. Disobedience is essentially a sin against love. For one to profess to love God and refuse to obey His commandments is not a sign of affection, it is a sign of hatred. Hatred and disobedience are equated in the thinking of the apostle.

The Lord made this clear when He spoke to the Pharisees, who considered themselves to be the sons of God. He told the parable of the man and two sons. The father told the first son to go, and he consented, but he did not go. He told the second son to go, and he refused, but then went out and did what his father had commanded. The Lord asked the Pharisees which of the two was truly the son of his father. Unable to escape the logic of our Lord's presentation, they replied that the true son was the one who did what the father commanded. Doing the will of God, rather than merely discussing it, is a proof of sonship.

The last phrase in verse 3, "His commandments are not burdensome," refers to our attitude toward the will of God and the Word of God. Many believers think that the will of God is something to be endured. They take up their cross and stumble along, crushed by the will of God. But John says the will of God is not burdensome. Submission to the will of God allows the grace of God to help us adapt to difficult circumstances.

In verses 4 and 5 John gives a third evidence of the new birth: the one born again overcomes the world.

> For whatever is born of God overcomes the world. And this is the victory that has overcome the world—our faith. Who is he who overcomes the world, but he who believes that Jesus is the Son of God?

Overcoming the world means that one manifests love of God and love of God's truth instead of the hatred displayed by the worldling.

John is not thinking here of the things that are in the world, things we so often characterize as being worldly. He is talking about the world's hatred of Jesus Christ. And the only way that one can rise above the attitude of the world, the only way one can rise above that basic sin nature with which he was born, is to walk by faith.

The Witness of the Spirit
1 John 5:6–12

When they were in the Upper Room, Christ promised the disciples that He would send the Holy Spirit, who would bear testimony to His works and to His person.

> However, when He, the Spirit of truth, has come, He
> will guide you into all truth; for He will not speak on
> His own authority, but whatever He hears He will speak;
> and He will tell you things to come. He will glorify Me,
> for He will take of what is Mine and declare it to you.
> (John 16:13–14)

In chapter 5 of his epistle John presents several witnesses to Jesus Christ. In the sixth verse he says the Spirit bears witness to Jesus because the Spirit is truth. And again in verse 8, "And there are three that bear witness on earth: the Spirit, the water, and the blood; and these three agree as one."

The Spirit's witness through *water* takes us back to Matthew 3, where John the Baptist presents a message to Israel, a people who had long been in darkness. "Repent, for the kingdom of heaven is at hand! . . . 'Prepare the way of the LORD; make His paths straight' " (Matt. 3:2–3). Many confessed their sin and were baptized in the Jordan. John's baptism was based on repentance—confessing sin and turning to righteousness. The Spirit has had an agelong ministry of reproving and rebuking— convincing people that they are sinners in need of salvation. In the ritual of the people of Israel, water signified cleansing; so John's baptism signified cleansing from sin. The ministry of the Spirit is first of all, then, to convince us that we are sinners and that we are in need of a Savior.

The Spirit bears testimony through *blood* that God has provided for human need. The Old Testament is encapsulated in the book of Hebrews: "Without shedding of blood there is no remission" (Heb. 9:22). Water could not take away sin; only blood can do this. That is why Peter wrote, you were not redeemed with corruptible things, like silver or gold, from your aimless conduct received by tradition from you fathers, but with the precious blood of Christ, as of a lamb without blemish and without spot. He indeed was foreordained before the foundation of the world, but was manifest in these last times for you. (1 Peter 1:18–20)

The Spirit convinces sinners that if they turn in faith to Jesus Christ and trust His blood, they will receive the gift of eternal life. Paul writes,

But when the kindness and the love of God our Savior toward man appeared, not by works of righteousness which we have done, but according to His mercy He saved us, through the washing of regeneration and renewing of the Holy Spirit, whom He poured out on us abundantly through Jesus Christ our Savior. (Titus 3:4–6)

God the Father also witnesses to Jesus. John speaks of this in verse 9: "If we receive the witness of men, the witness of God is greater."

God authenticated the person of Jesus at His baptism: "This is My beloved Son, in whom I am well pleased" (Matt. 3:17). On the Mount of Transfiguration, Peter, James, and John heard this authentication a second time (Matt. 17:5). The witness of the Father coincides with that of the Spirit—Jesus is the sinless One and His sacrifice avails for sinners.

Finally, John records that there is a witness within the child of God.

He who believes in the Son of God has the witness in himself; he who does not believe God has made Him a liar, because he has not believed the testimony that

God has given of His Son. And this is the testimony: that God has given us eternal life, and this life is in His Son. He who has the Son has life; he who does not have the Son of God does not have life. (vv. 10–12)

The eternal God fellowships with us by sharing His life with us. He invites us to share the security and the assurance that comes from believing Him.

QUESTIONS FOR REFLECTION AND DISCUSSION

Starting Points

1. Do you more often feel that you have overcome the world or are being overcome by the world?

2. When have you felt that God's will or His commands were burdensome? When have you found them to be a source of joy?

Exploring the Text

4. What does it mean to believe that Jesus is the Christ?

5. Do you think "His commandments are not burdensome" is a statement of fact or of attitude? Explain.

6. What do you think it means to overcome the world?

7. How do the Spirit, water, and blood bear witness to Christ?

Where Do We Go From Here?

8. How clearly are the three evidences of being born of God reflected in your life? What changes would you like to see?

9. How can you encourage someone who needs assurance of new life in Christ?

Lesson: 10

Till the End

"Knowledge is power," Sir Francis Bacon said in *Religious Meditations*. If so, the apostle John packs a lot of power into the close of his epistle. In the final nine verses he uses the word *know* no fewer than seven times.

John has confidence. He is assured. He knows. And we can, too.

Assurance of Eternal Life
1 John 5:13–15

John wrote his gospel to lead people to faith in the person of Jesus Christ, that through Him they might receive the gift of eternal life. To establish the validity of that gift John presented a number of Christ's miracles.

John's epistle gives us the witness of the Father and the Spirit to the person of Jesus Christ. The purpose of Gospel miracles and these witnesses in 1 John is the same—"that you may continue to believe in the name of the Son of God" (1 John 5:13).

John has another reason for writing this epistle: "That you may know that you have eternal life." John wrote to assure us that as soon as we believe on Christ we enter into eternal life.

There are multitudes today who have accepted Christ as Savior but who would have difficulty answering the question, "Are you saved?" They might reply, "I hope so." If asked, "Do you have assurance of eternal life?" they might reply, "No. I don't believe any person has the right to say he has eternal life. We must wait until we stand in judgment; only then will we know if we have eternal life."

What a tragedy that they do not rest in the promise of God that the one who receives Christ has eternal life the moment he believes. Failure to realize this has nothing to do with our eternal destiny, but it certainly affects our stay here on earth.

If one lives in fear and uncertainty, he cannot enter into the peace of God. What a comfort it is to know that, the moment we accept Christ as Savior, God shares His eternal life with us, and we become His partner. God has nothing to give us in eternity that we do not possess this very moment other than the experience of glory itself.

John has yet another assurance he wants to pass on: "This is the confidence that we have in Him, that if we ask anything according to His will, he hears us." God is accessible. This is peculiar to Christianity. In other religions God is inaccessible.

This is clearly revealed in the contest between Elijah and the prophets of Baal (1 Kings 18). Four hundred fifty prophets implored Baal to demonstrate that he was God by consuming their sacrifice with fire. But they had no assurance that in uniting their voices they could gain the attention of their god, so they leaped on the altar to attract his attention. They even cut themselves as though the bullock on the altar was not enough. What a picture of men futilely trying to arouse an inaccessible god!

How blessed we are that God is accessible. Jesus has opened the way into heaven and bids us, "Come to Me, all you who labor and are heavy laden, and I will give you rest" (Matt. 11:28).

The writer to the Hebrews also speaks of this:

> Seeing then that we have a great High Priest who has passed through the heavens, Jesus the Son of God, let us hold fast our confession. For we do not have a High Priest who cannot sympathize with our weaknesses, but was in all points tempted as we are, yet without sin. Let us therefore come boldly to the throne of grace, that we may obtain mercy and find grace to help in time of need.

Between God and the sinner was a barrier that no man could penetrate. After His death Christ, as our priest, parted the veil so that we were given free access to the presence of God. The Lord Jesus as our representative stands in the presence of God. Since He walked among men, He knows all of the weaknesses and burdens to which we are heir.

John tells us, "If we know that He hears us, whatever we ask, we know that we have the petitions that we have asked of Him" (1 John 5:15). John is assuring us that the God who hears will also answer prayer. God will respond to the cry of His child and will meet his need.

Prayer is an attitude of total dependence on God. Prayer is not pouring requests into the ear of God. God already knows the need. Prayer is consciously depending on God to meet our need in accordance with the promises of His Word. When the child of God depends on God, God's hand is moved.

Notice that John states, "If we ask anything according to His will, He hears us" (v. 14). Not every petition that the child of God presents to God is guaranteed fulfillment. When the child of God claims the promise of the Word of God as he prays to the Father, that prayer is certain to be answered. However, God gives no attention to what is prayed apart from the promises of His Word. For a prayer to be in accord with the will of God, it must be in harmony with the Word of God.

In daily life we accept the testimony of many people. A word of assurance from a salesman concerning his product encourages us to buy. How much more we should accept the assurance from God the Father and God the Spirit as they authenticate the offer of the Son.

Sin Leading to Death
1 John 5:16–17

Sin makes it impossible for a child of God to fellowship with his heavenly Father until the sin is confessed and he receives forgiveness. John has shown us in this epistle what fellowship involves and demands. Once again we see God's great concern about our fellowship with Him.

John here deals with sin in God's child and God's response to this sin. God divides the sins of His children into two classifications: sin which does not lead to death, and sin leading to death. In verse 16 John says, "If anyone sees his brother sinning a sin which does not lead to death, he will ask, and He will give him life."

What is a believer to do when he sees a fellow believer sin? He is to petition God. He is not told to ask for forgiveness, because the prayer of one believer cannot accomplish forgiveness for another. This prayer can move the hand of God to discipline the guilty party so that he will confess his sin and be restored to fellowship with God.

John promises that God "will give him life." John is not referring to the gift of eternal life. John is referring to the life of intimate fellowship that Jesus enjoyed with the Father while He was here on earth. John is saying that God will restore the erring believer to the intimacy of fellowship that was marred by his sin.

In verse 16 John gives us a sober and, to many, an unsettling word: "There is a sin leading to death." Many people are confused about what John is teaching because they equate sin leading to death with the unpardonable sin mentioned in Matthew 12. However, the two are quite different.

After Jesus had cast the demon out of a blind and mute man and enabled him to see and speak, the crowd said that only God could perform such a miracle. They were acknowledging that Jesus was who He professed to be—God's Son.

The religious leaders became frenzied when they heard this confession, and they ran among the people crying, "This fellow does not cast out demons except by Beelzebub, the ruler of the demons" (Matt. 12:24). They said Jesus was the son of Satan.

Jesus had been offering Himself to the covenant nation Israel as their Savior and as their king; He was calling on them to decide about His person. This Word of Jesus was substantiated by the miracles that the Holy Spirit produced through Him. The miracles Christ did were not His own, they were the Father's. The Father was testifying by the Spirit to the Word of the Son. There were two witnesses to Jesus Christ—His own testimony and the testimony of the Spirit through miracles.

If an individual accepted the testimony of Jesus, he did not need the miracles. By faith he came to salvation. If a person rejected the testimony of the Lord Jesus he might still he brought to faith by the testimony of the Spirit in miracles. But if he rejected the first witness, the

Word of Christ, and the second witness, the miracles of the Spirit, there were no further witnesses that God provided to lead men to faith in Christ.

So Jesus warned them:

> Every sin and blasphemy will be forgiven men, but the blasphemy against the Sprit will not be forgiven men. Anyone who speaks a word against the Son of Man, it will be forgiven him; but whoever speaks against the Holy Spirit, it will not be forgiven him, either in this age or in the age to come. (Matt. 12:31–32)

The Lord Jesus, then, is warning this generation that if they ignore His testimony and attribute miracles to the power of Satan, their fate is sealed, for God has no further witness to give them. They will be guilty of a sin that cannot be forgiven. That sin came to its consummation when the leaders in Israel said, "Crucify Him. . . . We have no king but Caesar!" (John 19:15). God judged Israel to be guilty of this sin when they crucified Jesus.

But John, in his letter, is talking about the sins of believers—those who have already accepted the testimony of Christ and the Spirit. What, then, did John have in mind when he said, "There is a sin leading to death"?

First of all, we must determine what kind of death John is talking about here. Is this physical or spiritual death? There are many who understand John to mean that there is a sin that will lead to spiritual death—the loss of salvation. But such an interpretation is contrary to the consistent teaching of the Word of God concerning the sins of those who trust Christ as their Savior.

In Psalm 103:12 the psalmist says, "As far as the east is from the west, so far has He removed our transgressions from us." In Isaiah 44:22 the prophet assures that God has "blotted out, like a thick cloud, your transgressions." Micah 7:19 states that God would cast sins into the depths of the sea, where no light can penetrate and where they can never be seen again. In Jeremiah 31:34 God says, "There sin I will remember no more." By an act of His will God can dismiss from His memory every sin that has been put under the blood of Christ. In Romans 8:1 Paul says, "There is therefore now no condemnation to those who are in Christ Jesus." John 5:24 states: "He who hears My word and believes in Him who sent Me has everlasting life, and shall not come into judgment, but has passed from death into life."

These are only a few of the many verses telling us that when our sins are covered by the blood of Christ they are dismissed from God's memory. The record is made clean, and there is no indictment lodged against us. If the phrase "There is a sin leading to death" meant that the guilty would lose their salvation, John would be denying the clear and consistent testimony of the Word of God. John cannot be writing about spiritual death. He is saying that there is such a thing as sin that ends in physical death.

Not all sin, John has told us, ends in physical death. But some sin may result in physical death. We have a number of illustrations in Scripture of sin leading to death. Nadab and Abihu, because of their rebellion, were consumed with fire (Lev. 10). Korah, his sons, and 250 priests were swallowed up into the earth (Num. 16). Ananias and Sapphira professed to give themselves totally to God and to the saints but God took their lives because their profession was a lie (Acts 5).

The purpose of these deaths was twofold: first, to bring the impenitent one to fullness of fellowship with God; second, to be a lesson to the saints of the peril of unconfessed sin. God does not regard broken fellowship lightly. To live with unconfessed sin is to invite discipline.

Many, no doubt, are asking, "If there is a sin leading to death, please tell me quickly what it is so that I can avoid it at any cost." John did not have a specific sin in mind. Any sin not confessed could result in a premature physical death for the child of God.

John says, "I do not say that he should pray about that" (1 John 5:16). The word translated *pray* is a different word from the word translated *ask* earlier in this verse. You will get the force of what John is saying if we read the latter part of verse 16 this way: "There is such a thing as sin leading to death. I do not say that he shall make inquiry about it." If a believer is near death but there is no evidence of unconfessed sin, we are not to ask, "What did he do to deserve this?" This presupposes that all sickness is the discipline of God for sin, but this is not biblical. We do not inquire about such matters, even if the individual dies. That is a matter between God and that individual.

God does not punish His children for their sins. Thank God for that! Punishment is retribution for wrong. Jesus bore the punishment for the believer's sin on the cross. God's purpose in discipline is stated twice in Hebrews 12. In verse 10 we read that He chastens for our benefit, "that we may be partakers [fellowshipers] of His holiness." The Father disciplines to restore us after a broken fellowship. Again in verse 11 we're told that "no chastening seems to be joyful for the present, but painful; nevertheless, afterward it yields the peaceable fruit of righteousness to those who have been trained by it." Thus righteousness is the product of fellowship.

John writes that God is so concerned about our fellowship with Him that He will use whatever means are necessary to restore us to fellowship. If His discipline is resisted, God's hand will become heavier and heavier until we are brought to confession. Should we fail to confess, God might remove us by physical death to bring us into that fellowship for which we were born again.

Lying in the Lap of Wickedness
1 John 5:18–21

Religion was designed to make worldly people otherworldly. James states, "Pure and undefiled religion before God and the Father is this: to visit orphans and widows in their trouble, and to keep oneself unspotted from the world" (1:27). There are two evidences of the validity of your faith: first, it produces a selfless love; second, it keeps you unspotted from the world.

John develops the same truths in 1 John 5:18–21. The first manifestation of the life of Christ is that we will love unselfishly. The second, our conduct will be so transformed that our lives will be patterned after another world.

When John says, "We know that whoever is born of God does not sin" (v. 18), he is not teaching that it is impossible for a born-again believer to sin. This would be contrary to the teaching of the Word of God, for there we have a record of saints who, although they possessed eternal life, did commit sin. John is instead emphasizing that the one who has been born of God has been given a new nature. The nature of God is imparted to the child of God and is incapable of committing sin.

While the child of God may operate at times by the old nature, it is no longer necessary for him to do so. The child of God sins only by refusing to operate by the new nature within him. Once it was necessary for us to live under the control of sin because we possessed only a fallen sin nature, but now we do this at the risk of divine discipline.

John explains why it is not necessary for the one born of God to live under the control of the old sin nature. He says, "He who has been born of God keeps himself, and the wicked one does not touch him" (v. 18). The word *keeps* suggests setting a guard. The child of God who lives by the new nature sets a constant guard over his thoughts, words, actions, and his patterns of life to see that they are not conforming to the world's dictates.

The Word of God charges the believer with responsibility for his conduct. It is not possible for us to excuse our sin by saying, "Satan made me do it." Satan may have been the tempter, but we are no longer obligated to submit to his enticements. Neither does the child of God have the right to say, "Everybody is doing it; I only conformed to the standards of the world in which I live." For we have been lifted out of the world by the new birth. If a child of God patterns his conduct according to the world, he denies the Spirit of God in him.

John describes graphically the state of the world. "The whole world lies under the sway of the wicked one" (v. 19). Or, "The whole world lies in the arms of the wicked one"! The worldling, like a baby, is being cradled by the evil one. He is also being fed by the evil one, so he will reproduce the devil's wickedness.

What is our safeguard against the world? "We know that the Son of God has come and has given us an understanding" (v. 20). We understand Satan's purpose and how he operates. The child of God puts himself on guard against being run in the mold of the world or "conformed," as Paul says in Romans 12:2.

Jesus was surrounded by the system of Satan, but He kept Himself from the world. His goals were never the goals that Satan works out through the worldling. His pattern of life was not the pattern of one who draws his strength from Satan. The things He held Himself responsible for were not what the world tells a man he ought to be doing. If we would enter into the fullness of life and experience the fullness of joy, we must be like the Lord Jesus.

John gives a concluding enjoinder. "Little children, keep yourselves from idols." What John had in mind is illustrated in the Old Testament. At the conclusion of forty years of wilderness wanderings, Israel was ready to enter into the land of promise. God gave a command to the children of Israel through Moses.

> Now the LORD spoke to Moses in the plains of Moab by the Jordan, across from Jericho, saying, "Speak to the children of Israel, and say to them: 'When you have crossed the Jordan into the land of Canaan, then you shall drive out all the inhabitants of the land from before you, destroy all their engraved stones, destroy all their molded images, and demolish all their high places; you shall dispossess the inhabitants of the land and dwell in it, for I have given you the land to possess. (Num. 33:50–53)

When the children of Israel came into the land, they were to remain disassociated from the idolatry of the people and from the false gods. As a people set apart, they were to destroy every idol and the high places devoted to their worship. Every remnant of idolatry was to be put out of the land.

God knew that if they removed the idols but left the idolaters, Israel would soon be corrupted. Therefore God said they were also to drive out all the inhabitants of the land. Why? Because idolatry will corrupt godliness, as God warned Israel:

> But if you do not drive out the inhabitants of the land from before you, then it shall be that those whom you let remain shall be irritants in your eyes and thorns in your sides, and they shall harass you in the land where you dwell. (Num. 33:55)

This is what John had in mind when he said to his children, "Keep yourselves from idols." There cannot be a marriage between the believer and the world. The believer cannot conform to the world and maintain the intimate life of fellowship with the Father. Fellowship with the Father demands complete separation from all that is in the world.

We were born into this world, but we were born again *out* of the world. We live in the midst of the world, but we need not be corrupted by the world. The child of God is held responsible to set a guard on his life so that the corruption of the world does not touch him. Only as we live the life of heaven in the midst of the world can we enjoy fellowship with the Father.

QUESTIONS FOR REFLECTION AND DISCUSSION

Starting Points

1. When have you most felt that you needed assurance of eternal life? Did you receive that assurance? If so, how?

2. How has the study of 1 John encouraged you to "continue to believe in the name of the Son of God" (v. 13)?

Exploring the Text

3. How do you experience assurance of your salvation? To what extent is it emotional? What other elements besides feelings are a part of assurance?

4. Why do you think so many people lack assurance? What would you say to someone who doubted his or her salvation?

5. Why don't we get everything we pray for? How do you explain verse 15?

6. What does John mean when he talks of a sin leading to death?

• •

7. What idols tempt Christians today?

Where Do We Go From Here?

8. What do you need to do personally to keep yourself from idols?

9. What is your usual reaction when you see a brother sinning? Is there anyone for whom you need to pray?

• •

Note to the Reader

The publisher invites you to share your response to the message of this book by writing Discovery House Publishers, P. O. Box 3566, Grand Rapids, MI 49501, U.S.A. For information about other Discovery House books, music, or videos, contact us at the same address or call 1-800-653-8333.